*12/4/12*

*To Mr. Rosenthal*
*I hope you'll*
*find the work*
*of value,*
*Sincerely*
*Jack Block*

Second Edition

# STUDYING AND WRITING HISTORY

## BY

## JACK BLOCK, Ph.D.

D1312440

Second Edition

# STUDYING AND WRITING HISTORY

## BY

## JACK BLOCK, Ph.D.

## HISTORY PUBLICATIONS

© Jack Block, 2006,  2009


Published By:

History Publications
Ridgewood, New Jersey 07450

Library of Congress
Catalog NUMBER: 72:151836

In memory of my mentor and inspirer, the late
Dr. Erling Hunt, Teachers College, Columbia University

# FOREWORD

When I was a very young man I entered the teaching profession as a high school history teacher. I immediately encountered a serious problem. Most of my students came into my classroom at the start of the school year with the firm belief that history is irrelevant and boring.

What to do? I had loved history as a student. To me, history was the story of flesh-and-blood people who lived exciting lives, who made world-changing decisions, and who were human just like me. Reading about them and their adventures was fascinating to me. I did well in history and relished the experience.

In my graduate history classes at Carnegie Mellon, Dr. Lisle Rose, my very favorite history professor, had suggested to us that most people are not able to fully appreciate history until they have a personal history of their own.

This made sense. To my students, the events of just ten years ago were ancient history. To me, these same events were significant happenings in my early teenage years, the topics of discussion in my own high school social studies classes. To my parents, these same ten-year-old events seemed as if they happened only yesterday, part of the fabric of their own recent lives.

How, then, to make history come alive for my students?

It finally dawned on me. In their science classes, my students learned scientific facts and theories, and then they conducted lab experiments to make those facts and theories come alive. At least for the short while they were in science classes, they became scientists.

In their literature classes, they enjoyed the works of great writers. Then they put their observations to work by composing essays and short stories of their own creation. In art classes they learned the theory of perspective, then put this knowledge to use by creating their own artistic renderings. In physical education classes they learned the theory of a sport such as tennis, then went out onto the tennis courts to try their hand at the performance aspect of the sport.

In subject after subject, I discovered, it was the same: My students had teachers who shared with them the important facts and concepts of their areas of study, and then actively engaged them in the doing of those subjects. This was true in every academic field. Except for history.

In their history classes, my students had heard lecture upon lecture. They had done their reading assignments, all focused on what appeared to be the certainties of past events and their meanings. And they had taken fact-based tests galore. History, therefore, appeared to my students to be a "done deal" -- all wrapped up long ago, with nothing left for them to discover, nothing for them to create.

No wonder they thought that history was boring. Holding his history textbook in his hand, one of my early students pointed out to me, with frustration and anger in his voice, that he didn't care about all the "stuff." "Why not," I asked. "Show me, Mr. B," he exclaimed. "Show me where I am, in this book! Show me, and I will memorize every word!" I could not.

There must be a better way to teach history, I thought. Not long afterward, I began the writing of a social studies textbook for high school students, a program that would put students into the center of the action. In classes using my textbook, students would actually have a chance to become a historian, a sociologist, an anthropologist, a geographer, a political scientist, an economist. They would learn by doing, not by memorizing and regurgitating disconnected facts.

It was at this juncture that, mercifully, I discovered Dr. Jack Block. His seminal work, **Understanding Historical Research: A Search For Truth**, became the essential underpinning of my history unit, and by extension, an important part of the philosophical framework of my entire textbook.

Dr. Block showed me through his writing, and later through his patient tutelage, how students at every level -- from elementary school through graduate school -- could make history come alive for themselves by actually sinking their teeth into the stuff of which historical accounts are made. Finally, here was an answer to my dilemma!

As I began using Dr. Block's insights and strategies with my own students, I saw the glaze in their eyes disappear, to be replaced with looks of wonder and excitement. Now, my students were finally able to see themselves in the historical accounts they, themselves, were creating. They were now debating the great issues of history with one another, instead of passively absorbing (some of) their teacher's lecture material. Lo and behold, history now became one of their all-time favorite subjects!

As you peruse this rich volume of new strategies and insights from Dr. Block, you will be tempted to use them all with your students. Take your time. Savor this volume as you would a fine meal of many different courses. Experiment with a few of these marvelous insights, adding them to your own repertoire of best practices, one at a time.

Your students will thank you for it.

John Jay Bonstingl
Columbia, Maryland

# PREFACE

When my first text was published, the computer, as we know it now was unavailable to the general public. Students and writers of history had to rely on libraries, generally, for sources of information and typewriters for the finished products of their works. Today, years later, the world of information has changed radically. The calculus of this change has been dramatic. Changes in computer technology, alone, have transformed the size of library collections. Imagine a computer which contains a database that may store an infinite number of sources of information. The language of the computer has given rise to such words and phrases as "the web," "internet," "database," "brain," "online, "e-mail," and a host of other words and phrases. The language continues to evolve at such a rapid rate as to change almost daily (Rodrigues, 2003, p.2). In spite of these changes, should you presently be interested in studying events or episodes which occurred more than fifty years ago, you will find it beneficial to examine sources located on library shelves. However, for more recent history, the computer will direct you to the location of recently published and non-published sources (Rodrigues, p.20).

As a student and writer of history, I have altered my approach to the study of history. Years ago, when I wrote Understanding Historical Research: A Search For Truth, I believed that history consisted of only one process. Now, with a Ph.D. in historical methodology and a doctoral dissertation on the subject, I realize that the study of history includes much more than historical research. It is my belief that this new text will demystify the processes of history and allow you, the reader, to engage in authentic, historical inquiry and will assist you in historical writing. This new work has been written for any one interested in writing history. Using historical sources, you will be able to write letters to and articles for newspapers, magazines, and electronic media. You will be able to create your memoir, examine family and community history, analyze current events reporting, take notes for autobiographical and biographical accounts, historical short stories, novels, and much more. When finished reading the text choose a topic of interest to you. Whatever your choice, this book is designed to guide you through your writing experience.

For both university and college professors, I suggest that your students either study this book as a separate unit or use it in conjunction with the required history textbook. It is most important to involve learners in the work of the historian. By using the same methodology and tools, students will discover that their history texts are launching pads that send them into the past in an educational detective game. Those who are taught the historian's tasks will find the study of history not only informative but rewarding. By learning the historian's approach to the writing of history, they will be able to use that approach themselves. It is for this reason that I have included an example of the writing of a former student. Ms. Michalski's paper appears at the end of Chapter IX, "Reaching Conclusions." In addition, I have added four different historical papers which I wrote for Dr. Hunt in his course, "The Study of History," in the graduate division of Columbia University

In all of my writing, I have tried to make the language "user friendly." In order to bring the material as close as possible to your experiences, I have made references to fictional accounts in schools. In some cases, I ask you, the reader, to pretend that you are attending school in order to observe and analyze sources of information. In content, I have focused attention on the needs of young adults because I believe that studying and writing history should not be postponed until one is enrolled at the graduate or doctoral level of education. Instead, I affirm that those who have mastered the secondary education curriculum have the ability to master the content of this book.

Jack Block
Ridgewood, New Jersey

# ACKNOWLEDGEMENTS

I wish to thank the following individuals at William Paterson University, Wayne, New Jersey: Professor Richard Kearney, Electronic Resource Librarian, encouraged me to write the chapter, *The Importance Of The Computer*." Anthony Joachim, Reference Librarian, created the outstanding cover for this text, the chart for the paper entitled, "*Coal Production in Pennsylvania for the Years, 1880-1900 at Ten Year Intervals. Graph and Design*," and the chart in Chapter IX, "*Reaching Conclusions*." In addition, he designed the graphics for the remainder of the text. Barbara Smith, Technical Library Assistant, prepared the entire manuscript for publication. I praise her for her diligent and meticulous work, boundless energy, sense of humor, and the many hours spent at home preparing this manuscript. Professor Ralph Malachowski proofread the manuscript with a full understanding of what I wanted to accomplish. I am grateful to him for his fine work.

I acknowledge Caryn Sobel for the outstanding work she did in putting together the index for the text. Although not affiliated with the university, she deserves the highest praise for her careful and painstaking attention to detail. In closing, I should like to express my appreciation to John Jay Bonstingl who graciously consented to write the forward to this book. The author of the popular text, Introduction To The Social Sciences, as well as several other books, Mr. Bonstingl is an international education consultant. He has worked with educators around the world.

# TABLE OF CONTENTS

# CHAPTER I

## STUDYING AND WRITING HISTORY

The term, "history," as used by the early Greeks, had the meaning of inquiry. It also stood for the reconstruction of past events (Mouly, 1978, p. 157). The word, "history," is more inclusive. Walsh has referred to it as the "...totality of past human actions and the narrative or account we construct of them now" (Walsh, 1967, p. 16). In an address delivered at the University of Berlin, Professor Mommsen asserted that history

> is nothing but the distinct knowledge of actual happenings, consisting on the one hand of the discovery, and examination of the available testimony, and on the other of the weaving of this testimony into a narrative in accordance with one's understanding of the men who shaped the events and the conditions that prevailed
>
> (Mommsen, Rectorial Address
> University of Berlin, 1874, translated
> By the editor, Stern, 1973, p. 192).

Some people believe that the study of history consists of dates and names. Others claim that history is a collection of facts. Still more report that it is the most boring subject offered by schools. Consider what history really is: the story of human life made up of actions, experiences, and ideas. What men and women have done, and have had done to them, what they have thought and said: This is history. The story of humankind is special. It is our story. Our thoughts and actions are the makings of history. What you believe, what you and your friends say, write, and think will be told one day by historians. They will be writing the history of your generation: its style, customs, habits, actions, and beliefs.

Why do we study the past? Why are we interested in understanding what men and women did before us, what they failed to do, what they felt, what they liked, and disliked? Perhaps, we just want to know why. We all have a past. We have roots or ties with those with whom we live and with relatives. We need to see ourselves not only as people, but as a society and as a nation. We must understand how we became the way we are. Only then, shall we understand where we are going. Only then, shall we understand the stream of history. Sometimes, we find that the truth hurts. We see that humankind has committed unspeakable crimes. Every now and then, an author distorts the truth so that it does not seem shameful in print. Yet, we observe at other periods the great and wonderful accomplishments that have benefited many people and not just a few.

The task of a historian is to examine the story of humanity and to interpret a page of the human record. The historian may either study the past by comparing it to the present or attempt to wipe the present from the mind and to explain the past by its own standards of conduct and behavior. This second approach is difficult because we may think that we act better and wiser than did previous generations of people. We have to fight our own conceit and prejudice. We may believe that we would never have acted the way people did in the Middle Ages nor even fifty years ago. Why did they not know better? Perhaps, we may say that they were foolish, foolish by our standards.

Recording events of the past and summarizing them into episodes is part of the function of a historian. However, what matters most to a writer of history is to understand the past and to interpret it for us. Understanding reasons for behavior and action helps to explain the true nature (origin) of behavior and action. The search for truth is a never ending goal. Although one scholar may have completed a study, perhaps, fifty or a hundred years later another historian will be investigating the same problem.

Historians are still trying to understand the reason for the assassination of President Lincoln. One scholar has wondered why a conspirator, when captured, was blindfolded and why his ears were clogged. Was there a group of Washingtonian politicians who wanted President Lincoln killed and Vice President Andrew Johnson convicted of treason (Eisenschiml, 1937, pp.173-176)?

At the time of the writing of the first draft of my original book, a shocking event occurred in the history of American life. President John F. Kennedy had been assassinated. During the writing of the second draft, his brother Senator Robert Kennedy and Reverend Doctor Martin Luther King, Jr. met similar fates. Investigations of these murders are still going on and much will be said and written by historians in the coming years. Perhaps, there may lie hidden from the press, radio, television, and the people of this nation some evidence that will not be revealed until all the participants in these horrible tragedies are long dead. Perhaps, some two hundred years from now, evidence will come to the surface, perhaps, never. Only time and research will tell.

Inspiration for the writing of this section of the chapter has come from the work of Professor Benjamin Bloom who invites his readers to develop their own classification system within their individual field of interest:

> Probably the most basic type of knowledge in a particular field
> contains a large number of symbols either verbal or non-verbal.
> These represent the basic language of the field--the shorthand
> used by workers in the field to express what they know
> (Bloom, 1956, p. 64).

What we refer to as the study of history is actually a combination of three processes taking place in a definite manner and directed toward a specific goal. Each process is unique and self-contained. As a student or writer of history, you are, perhaps, familiar with some or all of the terminology used in these processes. Let's examine each. The first process is called "historical research." What are the steps involved in this process? In the first step, you are looking for, trying to locate, or searching for sources of history. Why the prefix "re"? Normally, you are searching for information that has already been

2

located by one or more individuals. Otherwise, if no one else has ever seen or located the material that you have discovered, the process for you is historical search. After you have gathered the available sources, you are ready for the second step or operation which is classification of the sources of information. Classifying the material means labeling all evidence. Evidence is labeled as primary or secondary, or it is left in doubt. In a subsequent chapter you will read more about searching, researching, and classifying sources of information.

The second process in the study of history is called "historical method," "critical method," or "historical investigation." This set of operations includes the inspection, analysis, and evaluation of all sources of information. The historian uses a method to test and evaluate each piece of information. In a subsequent chapter about historical method of investigation, attention will be paid to the types of tests in the analysis of evidence. Upon completion of the analysis and evaluation of sources, the historian finishes the second process by establishing conclusions based upon the results of the tests. In sum, once you have begun to question the information that you have researched, you have begun the process of historical analysis also known as "historical method" or "critical method."

The third and final process of history is "historiography." The writing or telling of past events, episodes, or situations, "historiography" utilizes the processes of both historical research and historical method. The historian recreates the past by way of reconstruction and synthesis. These two operations will be discussed in another chapter. Suffice to say historiography is "… the imaginative reconstruction of the past from data derived by that process…and…the synthesizing of such data into historical exposition and narratives" (Gottschalk, 1969, pp. 48-49).

Photo courtesy of The Indiana Historical Society.

Sam Arnold is discussed in the work: <u>Why Was Lincoln Murdered</u>?
by Otto Eisenschiml, Little Brown & Company, published in 1937, page 176.
Although the book is out of print, one may still write to The General Lew Wallace
Study, Crawfordsville, Indiana for further information. Sam Arnold was one of
the defendants at the Lincoln assassination trial. What interest did General
Wallace have in the trial?

# CHAPTER II

## THE IMPORTANCE OF ACADEMIC DISCIPLINES

Once an event has taken place, it may not be repeated. One may not change completed actions from the past into unfinished scenes of the present. Life is not theatre; human beings are not actors rehearsing their parts day after day. Because of the impossibility of repeat performance, scientific experimentation during historical analysis is meaningless.

Although scientific testing is not possible, one may still reconstruct an event. How accurate and reliable the final shape of the model will be depends on many factors. The examination and piecing together of each part require skills of specialists trained in the behavioral, social, natural, and physical sciences.

We are all capable of assisting the modern historian because of the likelihood that we may be observers of some incident of historical importance. Our recollections, as such, may become valuable information. Whether we saw what actually took place or imagined what happened is a matter for the historian and other specialists to determine. Together, they act as a team. Their functions are to examine critically and to interpret the significance of each part of the model.

One member of the team who concentrates on feelings, attitudes, and behavior of all participants is the psychologist. He or she is also trained to interpret an event to which we may have been witnesses. According to the psychologist, our perception of what took place is based on factors of which we may be entirely unaware. These include our basic intelligence, body chemistry, personal as well as family history, and self-concept. Self-concept, for example, provides the psychologist with insight into what a person actually thinks of himself or herself. Are we as individuals proud or ashamed of what we have done to our own lives and to the lives of all those close to us? Whatever we think about ourselves will affect what we see, hear, and think about others. We may distort what we observe because of some hidden feeling or motive, such as jealousy, hatred, or love. In so doing, we may destroy or protect others involved in some incident.

The psychological approach is exciting because it personalizes history and reduces behavior of people to the understandable common denominators of human qualities and characteristics. Feelings, attitudes, self-concept, perceptions, basic intelligence, body chemistry, needs, and life experiences form the basic personality of each human being. We need to develop some understanding of the reasons for the behavior and actions of people in any historical age as we learn more about their personality development. Exploration of human personality is a natural pathway to studying and writing biographical history.

The anthropologist, another member of the team, analyzes habits, values, customs, and ideals: in short, the culture of the society to which the various participants belong. By the term, "culture," the anthropologist means the totality of learned behavior that is shared by most members of a tribe, community, society, or nation. This specialist may want to examine the findings of the psychologist in order to determine how much of the participants' behavior is due to their personality make up and how much is due to cultural conditioning. How has their culture molded their outlook on life, and therefore their perception of the world around them? For example, it would be extremely important to know if any prejudices these participants express had been formed by the early influences of their immediate families or by prejudices common to the community in which they have lived.

A problem arises as to how much personality is the result of biological factors or how much of what we are is the result of cultural conditioning. The anthropologist will argue that such habits as eating, cooking, cleaning and values of money, power, and success of the ideal man or woman are determined by the culture into which we have been born and raised.

In order to appreciate the work of the anthropologist, let us consider for a moment the culture of the American colonists. The anthropologist raises questions such as: What did these people value? What did they consider the good life? What values, attitudes, and knowledge did they hope to instill in their young? As participants in the colonial period, what pleasures, joys, sorrows, and fears did the early settlers experience in the wilderness of America? The answers to these questions not only shed light on the shared cultural experiences of this society but also help to increase understanding of human personality.

The sociologist will argue that within a given culture are included many groups, including immediate and fundamental groups which have most influence in shaping individual character and personality. This specialist helps the historian by narrowing the extent of influence of such groups as family, immediate neighbors, friends, and associates to whom members of a group owe allegiance and loyalty. The scholar has been trained to analyze perception and behavior in terms of group consciousness. He or she asks the following questions: How does a particular group of closely knit people view an event? Why does the group feel the way it does? How much does each member participate in the common experience? How much control does the group exert over each individual's actions and behavior?

The historian would do well to consider the sociologist's interpretations and answers to the above questions especially when social history is involved. Events normally occur in a group setting. So, it is important that the specialist most interested in the structure and character of a group, as well as the interaction of its members, share . knowledge and skills with the historian.

An economist sorts out information on topics such as standard of living, business, enterprise, and occupations in society. Primarily, this specialist examines needs and wants known as demands of society. The specialist relates demand to supply of available animal, vegetable, and mineral resources which are converted into economic goods and services with the aid of human, animal, mechanical, chemical, or electrical power. This scholar focuses attention on those goods and services which satisfy the demands of the people. Of course, the economist realizes that economic "wants," such as a color television set or college education are, also, culturally determined. This is why the economist is interested in the work of the anthropologist.

The economist also considers totals of production, distribution, and consumption of all goods and services. One notices rates of change in how quickly or slowly goods are made, sent to stores to be sold, and purchased by the population. One classifies goods as "consumer" or "capital." Although consumer goods are used directly by the public, capital goods usually remain in factories. Goods such as machines are considered capital goods because they are used to produce or manufacture consumer products. On the other hand, "services" help to keep goods and all living matter in working or healthy condition. As examples, the gas station attendant performs a service for the automobile driver. The doctor and lawyer perform other services no less important for the public.

The interpretations formed by our specialists are helpful to the historian as he or she begins to reconstruct a particular event or series of events in which one may see economic, cultural, sociological, and psychological forces which govern the actions of participants. To illustrate: During the American colonial period much of Catholic Europe wanted fish for Friday meals. This cultural, religious, social, and psychological "want" was soon transformed into an economic "need" or "necessity." Demand for fish was efficiently satisfied by supply due to the establishment of the New England fishing industry which grew and prospered as a result. Governments in both colonial America and England encouraged and supported this industry.

A historian is constantly faced with problems which are the domain of the political scientist. Some people believe that this specialist studies government. Other people report that this specialist studies politics. Still more claim that his or her function is to analyze power and influence in any society. Dr. Gibson, a former political scientist at Tufts University, has broken down into six parts the topics which his field of inquiry explores. He calls these the six elements in the governing process of society.

| | | |
|---|---|---|
| 1. | Governed- | People |
| 2. | Rulers - | Some authority |
| 3. | Politics - | Process whereby rulers come to occupy some position of authority |
| 4. | Government - | The framework (rulers may come and go; the institutional framework stays) |
| 5. | Policy Making Process - | By vote, by hand, by written choice, etc. |
| 6. | Policy- | Domestic or foreign, inter/intrastate or tribal |

From a speech delivered by Dr. John Gibson, summer workshop, Educational Services Inc., Cambridge, MA, 1964.

The political scientist assists the historian by examining each of these elements and by relating them to the particular locale in which the event or events under consideration have taken place. The political scientist is very concerned with how the governing process has affected the behavior and actions of members of the community. It is important to examine the interpretations of the other specialists in order to focus attention on the question of how governmental policies have helped or hindered participants in their desire to satisfy their needs and wants. In the example given of the growth of the fishing industry, the political scientist may wish to investigate those governmental policies which encouraged the development of this enterprise.

The biologist and ecologist have a unique working relationship. Whereas, the biologist is concerned with the origin, structure, growth, and reproduction of all living matter, the ecologist is primarily interested in studying the adaptation of human life to the environment. Both specialists help the historian because each is interested to a degree in human adaptation. They are concerned with such questions as: How do the participants keep themselves alive? How well have they been able to grow, reproduce, and adjust to the strains of a constantly changing environment?

The ecologist has looked at war, pestilence, and other forms of human suffering and their affects on the course of history. He or she helps the historian when each focuses attention on the ever changing environment and its influence on the anatomy, or on the physical and emotional endurance of humankind. The ecologist, also, assists in examining a particular group's attempts at cooperation with other population groups or its struggles and competition for land and natural resources. He or she may wish to analyze the group's potential for acts of aggression such as warfare as a solution to its problems.

Equally helpful to both historian and ecologist is the geographer. With the geographer's knowledge of "topography," meaning land and surface features, he or she may direct attention to topics of climate, soil, vegetation, population, land use, and any other available resources within the area under study. The geographer helps the historian identify those resources, such as minerals and water which may be available for use in the locale. While both anthropologist and economist examine needs and wants which affect land usage, the geographer has a different approach, one that gives added insight into human motives and intelligence. He or she observes how geography has shaped culture and how culture has changed geography.

Perhaps, more than any other member of the team, the archaeologist is interested in articles of past societies. Considering a historical event or series of events under discussion, this specialist searches for any relics and artifacts used by participants. Tools, household appliances, mechanical devices for home and work, and mementos tell something about the technology of that society. Thanks to the contribution of the archaeologist, the historian is able to better understand the use made of a discovered object and the importance attached to it by those living during the time period under discussion.

A rather complicated but gratifying process performed by the archaeologist is the placing together of all discovered items into groups depending on such factors as age and usage of items.  Since it is likely that he or she will find buried together remains of past and present civilizations, the archaeologist has a difficult task separating and dating the evidence found.  The dating of artifacts is difficult because these artifacts may have lost some of their original shape or chemical composition.  Time, weather, and other destructive forces have their damaging effects on such items.  Some materials, when unearthed, require care in handling because of the likelihood of their disintegration by oxygen in the air.

At this point, an archaeologist often needs the advice of a chemist.  By examining samples of those items, the chemist is able to determine the content and age of the materials.  By such examination, the chemist may also be able to tell whether or not relics are authentic.  In order to preserve very old evidence, it is important that the chemist single out any elements which are harmful to the composition of the artifacts.  This specialist may advise an archaeologist how to preserve these remains.  When we consider the likelihood of future explorations on other planets, the chemist will be of great service to the exploring teams.

Frequently, the historian needs to turn for additional support from the specialist who studies natural laws, properties, states of non-living matter, and energy.  This specialist is the physicist.  He or she may help by identifying the nature and extent of atmospheric pressures and pulls which may do harm to some physical remains.  With specialized knowledge of mechanical force, he or she is able to explain how a particular machine was used.  The physicist is also trained to advise the historian on the extent of electrical and atomic power used by the participants.  Based on the design and construction of such finds as sections of bridges or buildings, the physicist may ascertain the extent of the participants' mathematical or scientific abilities.  The historian may benefit from the physicist's interpretation of technological development of the society under investigation.  By examining the society's use of animal, human, machine and electric power, both specialists may appreciate what humankind has accomplished because of understanding of physical laws and properties.

The modern historian may benefit from the talent of the journalist.  Because of the contribution of this specialist, a scholar may become interested in an article which has appeared in some chronicle or magazine and will realize some historical value in the article.  Also, because of the journalistic style of writing, the public is likely to become interested in the topic and may demand that more research be done about a particular event and its participants.  By writing about the work of specialists, the journalist is able to inform the public of the contribution that the whole team makes to historical methodology.

The writer or literary specialist, like the journalist, is a most important assistant to the historian.  Because of the specialist's creative talent, he or she brings an episode to the attention of many different kinds of audiences.  Playwrights or dramatists, poets, biographers, essayists, novelists, and literary critics may select historical topics for their audiences and readers.  Very often, the literary specialist will take upon himself or herself the responsibility of doing research in order to use available sources from the past.  The hours spent in study, in interviewing participants, and in examining records of contemporaries could be of value to the historian. However, because of freedom of expression given the writer, his or her point of view may differ widely from that held by the historian. Nevertheless, it is up to the historian to examine the writer's interpretation because it is the historian who should determine the historical worth of the literary specialist's portrayal of history.

If there are any members of the team who question the meaning of human life, they are philosophers and theologians. These specialists go beyond all others in trying to analyze and interpret what the participants feel is their purpose in living in the society under examination. It is to philosophers and theologists the historian will turn for answers to questions such as these: What makes their lives worth living? What is beauty? Is there love in their society, and for whom? How does their culture teach them right from wrong? How do they explain the unexplainable? That is, do they believe in a religion or divine spirit which guides them along a definite path? What is truth to these people and how do they explain such a concept?

Before the close of this chapter, two comments are necessary. First, there are specialists whose contributions have not been considered. Since some point of view is necessary by this writer regarding the choices made, let it suffice to say that in his opinion, the previously mentioned specialists assist the historian most in his or her daily tasks.

Second, just as historians do not always agree on an interpretation of a historical happening, other specialists, also, have conflicting interpretations among their colleagues. For example, one psychologist's explanation may differ from another's regarding behavior and actions of participants in an event. However, both psychologists add to the dimensions of the reconstruction.

What makes the contributions of disciplines exciting is that many specialists are involved in the creation of a work of art. Therefore, we have people cooperating to determine what interpretations are most correct and beneficial. The reader is, then, stimulated by the knowledge that those specialists have met and used their minds and skills to make a valid and worthwhile contribution to the processes of history.

## FOR FURTHER STUDY

Choose a historical figure and try to trace the personality development of the individual. How much material is available on your topic?  Here are some examples:

       (a)      Pre-World War I Royal Families

       (b)      Samuel Adams

       (c)      Henry VIII

       (d)      Thomas Paine

Consider other specialists who have not been mentioned in this chapter and who assist the modern historian.  In what ways does each help the scholar?

Think of news items which have become subjects of research during the past two to five years.  What did the original article state?

How may an art historian and musicologist assist the historian?

The following photographs show examples of how the archaeologist handles human remains:

Egyptian, Dynasty XVIII. Thebes, Valley of the Kings, Tomb of King Tut-ankh-amun.
View of The entrance to tomb of Ramesses VI and Tomb of Tut-ankh-amun Metropolitan
Museum of Art (TAA2). Photography by Egyptian Expedition, The Metropolitan
Museum of Art.

Egyptian, Dynasty XVIII. Thebes, Valley of the Kings, Tomb of King Tut-ankh-amun; Carter and A.R. Callender wrapping up one of the two statues of the King in the antechamber for removal from Tomb. The Metropolitan Museum of Art (TAA715). Photography by Egyptian Expedition, The Metropolitan Museum of Art.

**13**

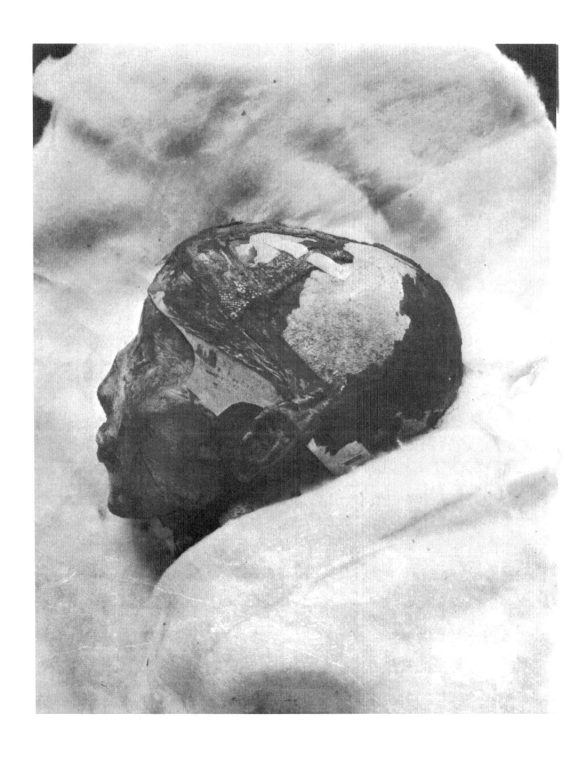

Egyptian, Dynasty XVIII, Thebes, Valley of the Kings, Tomb of King Tut-ankh-amun.
Head of mummy, side view.  The Metropolitan Museum of Art (TAA535). Photography
by Egyptian Expedition, The Metropolitan Museum of Art.

**14**

# CHAPTER III

## IN SEARCH OF TRUTH

In the play, <u>Hamlet</u>, Polonius gives the following advice to his son: "This above all, to thine own self be true, and it must follow as the night the day thou canst not then be false to any man." Polonius is not considered a wise man and yet his words to his son are often quoted as words of wisdom. Indeed, it would be ideal if one could be completely truthful with oneself and, in turn, completely truthful with other people.

"Truth" is very difficult to define. What is truth to one person may be falsehood to another. It is this aspect of truth which the student and writer of history must consider in the search for accuracy when analyzing events of the past.

Those people who recorded occurrences along the road of human history were, first and foremost, human beings possessing their own points of view, prejudices, biases, and purposes. No one is entirely free from such human frailties. In any discussion of history, the historian must consider not only the "facts" as reported by the original recorder of the event, but also the character and personality of the recorder.

For example, examine an account of the American Revolution written by the recorder. Pretend that it is a contemporary report of a battle during the war between the American colonists and the British army. The person who is recording the event is there and reports what he or she sees, hears, and feels. What greater authority may be found to describe what went on? None! But there are matters which we must consider as we read the version of the battle.

Let us start by asking whether the person was a patriot or a loyalist? Was he or she viewing the battle as a hopeful American fighting for personal liberty and freedom from the tyranny of the English throne? Was the person a British subject fighting against rebellion and in support of the sovereignty of King George III? Do you see how the reporter's point of view might have affected what he or she saw, heard, and felt at that time? Do you understand how that person's record of the events might have been influenced by his or her own psychological state of mind? What might have been a glorious victory in one report might have been recorded as a dismal failure in another.

The personal account of the same battle may also be influenced by the bias and prejudice of the source. Although bias and prejudice are learned, they are not easily controlled. The most objective reporter of an event may not be able to keep personal bias or prejudice from affecting what he or she sees, hears, and feels. If the person recording the battle had a fundamental admiration for uniforms, military order, and correct battle procedure, the recorder might have injected into the account of the battle bias for the British troops and prejudice against the ragged soldiers of the colonial army. If the recorder admired individual courage and "underdogs," that person might have expressed bias in support of the farmer-soldiers of America and prejudice against the trained and superior soldiers of England.

Also to be considered in evaluating historical reports is the purpose of the person recording the event. If the recorder at the scene of the battle were British and were writing the account for the people back in England, the recorder could have chosen to report only those events which would make readers optimistic. He or she could have chosen to eliminate information which would put the British army at a disadvantage. If the recorder were a colonist, that person could have reported those events which would have emphasized the bravery or cleverness of the Americans. The viewer could have decided to eliminate the losses and fatalities in order not to demoralize the American public. These ideas of emphasis and elimination of "facts" for a purpose often distort history.

Our picture of the American Revolution, as an example, is much different from the one you may read in an English history book. In the United States, the American Revolution is considered a glorious confrontation that was responsible for the formation of our country. It is described as a series of battles between the trained and experienced troops of an unfair tyrant determined to keep free people as colonial subjects, and a disorganized and inexperienced group of courageous patriots just as determined to gain liberty for themselves and for their children despite the odds against them. In American classrooms, we cheer their victory. In England, the American Revolution is considered a minor insurrection of a group of ungrateful traitors who were permitted to win after several skirmishes because England had more important battles in Europe at that time. Which version is the correct one? The student of history should be aware of both and should try to sift the truth from as many accounts as one finds. One should consider at all times the points of view, biases, prejudices, and purposes of the various accounts. Perhaps, there is some truth on each side.

There is another aspect in the search for truth which affects you and your view of historical events. If you are to use the processes of history, you must also consider yourself: your point of view, your bias, your prejudice, and your purpose. Just as the contemporary viewer brings subjectivity to history, so you, as a student of history, may have difficulty in remaining completely objective. In writing an account of a historical event, are you guilty of selectivity? Are you willing to consider ideas and information that conflict with your pre-conceived notions of the event? Have you decided beforehand what you want to prove? Do you have prejudices which make you discount information from a particular source? Do you prefer one version of an event over another? Are you willing to consider all sides of a controversy?

Dig deeper in the search for truth. Have you ever wondered why we hide our true feelings and thoughts from one another? In our everyday interpersonal relations, our dealings with others, we should ask ourselves, "Of whom or of what am I afraid?" As you observe your own family, try to understand why family members may keep secrets from one another and from you. Each family member has the same basic rights as you: the right to keep silent, the right to pretend, and the right to bury the past.

If we penetrate further in our search, we may come across a tape recording of a family discussion. What may we hear? Perhaps, some bias and prejudice may come to the surface of conversation. We may hear a discussion in which some relative swears that what he or she did or said is the truth. Who is telling the truth? Who is lying to the group and to oneself? If we admit to misunderstanding, conflicting versions of truth, or lack of respect for the opinions of members of our own families, how do we expect to understand, believe, or interpret the experiences of other families, societies, and nations?

Expanding our search to include the family as a group, we should ask whether or not families are always truthful in their dealings with other families in their community. Why? Why not? Could families be completely open with outsiders? There are family matters which are considered private. They are, therefore, closed to the outside world. Unfortunately, by not discussing problems openly with other people, some family groups may become lost in hopeless battles of hate, prejudice, and misunderstanding that widen the gulf between people.

In an attempt not to face itself and to withdraw from the process of self-understanding, a family or any other group may do what an individual does. It may look at itself in a mirror and see only what it wants to see. It may protect its members from ugly truths which it is not ready to face. It may project its hatred and dishonesty on to other families or groups by saying that these other people are the real "bad apples" in the community. It may say collectively, "That other family, not ours, is the prejudiced one in town. Our family does not dislike them. They dislike us!" Actually, the first family has not been able to examine itself truthfully. The root of the problem may lie <u>within</u> it rather than <u>outside</u> of it.

As we examine our relationships with outsiders, we should ask ourselves: Do we really know one another at all? Do we actually see one another, hear one another, or understand one another? Do we say "Yes," when we actually mean, "No!"? Do we talk <u>at</u> one another and not <u>with</u> one another? In our relations with people we often build images of others and we imagine that we really understand these people. We observe their behavior carefully at a certain time and place. We formulate a complete appraisal or generalization without ever giving these people opportunities to demonstrate different forms of behavior. Finally, we say, "We know them." Do we? Will we ever know others <u>truthfully</u> that way?

Let us apply these same questions to our study of international relations. We may say of an adversary, for example, that he or she is brutal or vicious. Do we really know the enemy? Do we know what this individual may be like at home with family? On the battlefield the person may react one way. At home, in an atmosphere of love, peace, and security, the individual may become another person. The tragedy for humanity is that we may never know this individual's true self.

"To thine own self be true…." To see faults in others but to ignore those faults in ourselves; to magnify faults in others and to dismiss our own are actions which are inexcusable in human relations and in historical methodology. Because we are human, we may be blind to our true selves. Our goal should be to remove the causes of our blindness and to develop insight, the ability to see the hidden motives for our behavior.

Above all, what seems to be missing in the search for truth is empathy for others. By becoming an understanding person, you are able to put yourself "in the shoes," so to speak, of another. You establish an empathic relationship by making such remarks as, "I know how you feel. You feel that…." You are showing the other person that you know or are trying to learn how he or she feels. You also show that you understand the experiences through which another person is going without that person having to tell you. What is most important about the empathic relationships you establish is that each involvement helps you to become more truthful to yourself. You come to know yourself better because you become involved with feelings, emotions, and experiences of others.

How may the concepts described above (which have dealt with the reader) be applied to the historian? The writer of history must face himself or herself when writing about the past in the very same way each of us must face our self, truthfully. We depend upon the historian to do the work well. Studying the past means unlocking doors, examining secrets and mysteries of the past, and attempting to uncover hidden feelings of those who lived before us.

The sources of information which humankind left to its heirs and to historians represent the reflection of people's lives that they saw when they looked into their mirrors. Why did they choose to preserve certain records, papers, letters, and mementos, and not others? What did those people of the past want us to know or to find out? What did they wish to bury forever? We should ask ourselves when we consider history, "What is truth?" Did the people of yesterday see themselves any more or less truthfully than we see ourselves?

The reason for asking you to consider conflicting versions of truth in family discussions is to prepare you to consider the same problems that exist for the historian. How may we expect the historian to be open-minded and objective about the past if we are not always open-minded and objective with ourselves and our families? Is it fair to ask the modern scholar to make judgments about the past? How may one judge accurately, impartially, and truthfully when we may be unwilling to judge daily events and experiences without taking sides? You may answer by saying that the historian writes about those who lived long ago. The scholar is unlikely to be biased or prejudiced in judgment since he or she could not have known these people of yesterday. If the historian is a descendant of a particular group will the scholar take its side in a battle, cause, or moral issue? Will he or she favor one side over the other because of national, religious, ethnic, or racial bias? The historian may be entirely unaware of this feeling. However, bias or prejudice may in one way or another influence thoughts and writing.

The historian is faced with such a limited number of sources of information as compared to the totality of unrecorded human experiences that he or she may become a prisoner of those sources. How may one be sure that one is not misinterpreting the statements, feelings, and actions of those individuals, families, or groups which the scholar is studying? In addition, if the historian admits that he or she is unable to explain the past because the past does not make any sense, will you accept that admission?

Whatever conclusions the historian draws may offend someone. As in the case of generalizations drawn about our enemy, one may do the same with a generalization about a historical figure. One historian may work on a positive characteristic of an individual's personality, while another completely overshadows such a trait with a negative portrait of the same individual. A third historian may write with humility about an aspect of human life of the past because that writer honestly or truthfully sees the same conduct or weakness in his or her own world and surroundings. A fourth historian may condemn some aspect of conduct in the past and may not admit that the present generation of which he or she is a part is guilty of similar wrongdoing. To see and to magnify faults in others while ignoring those faults in ourselves is inexcusable not only in human relations but also in the writing of history.

The study, interpretation, and writing of history require empathy on the part of the historian. The scholar should be prepared to look at the past open-mindedly, sympathetically examining individual and group needs and aspirations. The historian should think, "I know how you people of the past must have felt. You worked hard and suffered because…." Whatever they thought or felt the scholar should respect their view of life. The historian should be humane. At the same time he or she should help humanity to rediscover these people and to know them more deeply and truthfully.

The writer of history must develop an inquiring mind. The scholar must constantly question his or her reasons and motives for studying a certain portion of history. One must ask oneself, "What are my intentions?" Is the writer interested in seeking truth? What is it one wishes to prove? An inquiring mind is always open to new ideas, suggestions, and information. So, the historian asks questions and challenges accepted practices or ideas. Referring to the state motto of Missouri, the scholar imagines, "I am from Missouri. You have got to show me!" One learns to stop believing everything one sees, hears, or reads without questioning the accuracy and reliability of the information. One must search for the hidden bias and prejudice within oneself as well as within the information one holds. Above all, the historian must be willing to change a point of view, an attitude, or an opinion in search of truth.

In summary, it would be ideal to be able to prove that old Polonius was, indeed, wise. As present day writers of history make inroads into the human quality which enters all historical data, it is just possible that the historian of the future will be able to recognize and analyze genuine truth. With knowledge of self, expanded to awareness of human frailty, it may happen that "…to thine own self be true, and it must follow as the night the day thou canst not then be false to any man." will become a way of life not only for the historian but for humanity as well.

## FOR FURTHER STUDY

On the following page you will see a copy of Thomas Jefferson's early draft of the Declaration of Independence. This copy, a photo, courtesy of the Library of Congress, includes a protest against the slave trade. Why did Jefferson remove this portion from the final draft of the Declaration of Independence?

↑ abolishing our most valuable ~~important~~ Laws

for taking away our charters & altering fundamentally the forms of our governments

for suspending our own legislatures & declaring themselves invested with power to

legislate for us in all cases whatsoever:

he has abdicated government here, [by declaring us out of his protection & waging war against us. withdrawing his governors, & declaring us out

of his allegiance & protection:]

he has plundered our seas, ravaged our coasts, burnt our towns & destroyed the

lives of our people:

he is at this time transporting large armies of ↑scarlet and other↑ foreign mercenaries to compleat

the works of ~~death~~ desolation & tyranny already begun with circumstances ↑scarcely paralleled in the most barbarous ages, & totally↑

of cruelty & perfidy unworthy the head of a civilized nation:

he has ↑he has incited treasonable insurrections, excited domestic insurrections amongst us, and has↑ endeavored to bring on the inhabitants of our frontiers the merciless Indian

savages, whose known rule of warfare is an undistinguished destruction of

all ages, sexes, & conditions [of existence:]

[he has incited treasonable insurrections of our fellow ~~citizens~~, with the

allurements of forfeiture & confiscation of our property:

he has ↑he has constrained others ... on the high seas ... to bear arms against their ... to become the executioners of their friends & brethren↑ waged cruel war against human nature itself, violating it's most sa-

-cred rights of life & liberty in the persons of a distant people who never of-

fended him, captivating & carrying them into slavery in another hemi-

-sphere, or to incur miserable death in their transportation thither. this

piratical warfare, the opprobrium of infidel powers, is the warfare of the

Christian king of Great Britain. determined to keep open a market

where MEN should be bought & sold, he has prostituted his negative

for suppressing every legislative attempt to prohibit or to restrain this

~~determining to keep open a market where MEN should be bought & sold:~~

execrable commerce↑: and that this assemblage of horrors might want no fact

of distinguished die, he is now exciting those very people to rise in arms

among us, and to purchase that liberty of which he has deprived them,

by ~~murdering the people~~ upon whom he also obtruded them: thus paying

off former crimes committed against the liberties of one people, with crimes

which he urges them to commit against the lives of another.]

in every stage of these oppressions" we have petitioned for redress in the most humble

terms": our repeated petitions have been answered ↑only↑ by repeated injuries". a prince

whose character is thus marked by every act which may define a tyrant", is unfit

to be the ruler of a people ↑free↑ [who mean to be free". future ages will scarce believe

that the hardiness of one man", adventured within the short compass of twelve years

↑only↑ to lay a foundation so broad & undisguised for tyranny

over a people fostered & fixed in principles

of ~~liberty~~. freedom]

# CHAPTER IV

## THE IMPORTANCE OF THE SCIENTIFIC METHOD

There are many differences between the scientific and historical methodologies of inquiry. Despite these differences, there are important similarities between the two. If we apply the scientific method to the study of history we attempt to make the historian as exacting, persevering, and objective as the scientist. We ask the historian to test the evidence, which are the sources of information, according to internationally recognized methods of analysis. We expect the evidence to be tested for credibility and reliability. In other words, given the same sources of information and same method of testing those sources, will any other historian studying the same evidence come to the same conclusions as our first historian? Finally, we expect that the conclusions will have been based upon utmost objectivity of the historian.

It is necessary to define "objectivity." Writers explaining the processes of history invite their readers to examine all sources of information and "...to penetrate them to the bottom of their existence and to portray them with complete objectivity" (Von Ranke, 1885, reprinted, 1973, p. 42). Garraghan has used the term, "objectivity," together with the truth as he states

> Zeal for the truth and objectivity are in reality only different aspects of the same ideal in history. By objectivity (or the virtually equivalent term, impartiality) is meant such a detached and neutral attitude in the historian as enables him to deal with his material in the light of the evidence alone
>
> (Garraghan, 1946, pp. 46-47).

Using the scientific method as our model for the study of history, we begin by examining a problem or condition in society that had or has existed, a problem that interests us. The need to solve the problem comes from the historian or scientist and those people who believe the problem is worth the time and effort to undertake such work. For example, suppose we have two problems, one facing the scientist and the other facing the historian. For the scientist, the example is the following: There is a growing population of older people who are living longer lives in the United States. This condition leads the scientist to ask, "How may these people maintain a healthy life in their later years of life?"

For the historian, the example may be the problem of prejudice, persistent racism, and religious, or ethnic hatred in American culture. These problems have led some historians to examine the source of prejudice within our society and culture. For example, what was the condition of this prejudice during the 1920s?

The isolation of a problem leads both scientist and historian to focus on relationships from which they both pose questions. In the case of science, is there a relationship between diet and longevity? In the case of history, was there a relationship between anti- Catholic prejudice at the national Democratic Party convention of 1924 and the candidacy of Al Smith? These questions of relationships lead to the next step in the scientific method, the formulation of a hypothesis. A "hypothesis" is defined as a provisional, tentative, or working assumption or explanation (Gottschalk, 1969, p. 142; Garraghan, 1946, p. 153; Shafer, 1969, p. 143; Val Dalen, 1973, p. 176; Johnson, A., 1926, p. 167; Hockett, 1955, p. 8). The statement of hypothesis follows: for science, the affect, impact, or influence of diet on health and longevity; for history, the affect, impact, or influence of anti-Catholic prejudice at the Democratic convention of 1924 on the candidacy of Al Smith.

Once both scientist and historian have stated their hypotheses, they are obligated to define all terms within the hypotheses. How does one define such words as "diet," "health," "longevity," or "prejudice," "Democratic convention," and "candidacy"? How does each scholar plan to use these words? Anyone wishing to examine the hypotheses will have a clear understanding of what the scientist and historian have in mind. Also, certain words within each hypothesis are measurable or quantifiable. They are called "factors" or "variables" because they may vary in measurement or quantity. One may measure the amount of food in the diet. One may count the number of anti-Catholics who voted against the nomination of Al Smith because of religious prejudice.

In both science and history, the hypothesis accomplishes several tasks. It sets the stage for actual investigation, experiment, and testing. It defines and limits the study. It prepares the way for anyone interested in the study to use the same hypothesis offered in the initial study to support the original conclusions. The hypothesis may be disputed by the results of a second study which may reduce the reliability of the conclusions offered by the initial study. Whatever the case, the hypothesis prepares the scientist for experimentation and the historian for reconstruction after analysis of sources. At this point, there is a clear separation between science and history.

The scientific method demands that the scientist experiment directly. Whatever the hypothesis, the scientist manipulates materials he or she uses in an experiment and repeats the experiment as many times as is necessary in order to obtain consistent results. By observing and taking notes during each experiment, the scientist is able to record happenings and results. If differing occurrences take place, the scientist is able to take note of variation of condition and results. By comparison, in the case of history, the historian has no power to experiment. The historian studies past events which may not be repeated for experimental purposes. Direct experimentation is not possible. By examining the available sources of information, the historical investigator tests those sources of information, draws conclusions, and then reconstructs the event. By examining the sources, the historian is able to observe what took place. However, that is not direct but indirect observation. The process of reconstruction takes place after the careful analysis of all sources. Suffice to say that when all the factors and variables have been carefully analyzed and tested, the historian puts all the pieces together and is then able to establish conclusions.

Both scientist and historian develop conclusions based upon the evidence presented. Both professionals, essentially, ask the same questions. Do the conclusions drawn from the experiment or reconstruction of events support the hypothesis? If so, to what extent or to what degree? If not, why not? It is essential to point out that in both the scientific and historical methods, the conclusions do not necessarily have to support the hypotheses. The reason is that in science as in history, objectivity is most important. Conclusions should be based upon accurate and objective investigation and recording of the findings.

Finally, both scientist and historian must develop interpretations based upon the conclusions that were stated. The interpretations of both the scientific and historical methods are the final products. They may be in written form or lecture. This section of the historical processes will be further explained in the chapter, "Historiography." In closing, it is fitting to remember the great historian, von Ranke, a 19th century German historian who believed that history should be studied scientifically and who wanted his students to apply the rules of the scientific method to their hypotheses. Especially, he wanted the past presented as it was (Von Ranke, 1885, Introduction).

# CHAPTER V

## THE IMPORTANCE OF INVESTIGATIVE METHODOLOGIES

In Chapter Four, I referred to the importance of "Scientific Methodology," commonly known as the "Scientific Method" in studying and writing history. You will recall that the operations of scientific methodology are as follows: presentation of a problem to be solved, creation of a hypothesis, definition of terms, location and analysis of evidence, experimentation and testing of variables and factors within the hypothesis, development of conclusions, and interpretations based upon objective findings. In studying and writing history, how may you apply the scientific method? Suppose you have an interest in a sport such as baseball. How may the scientific method guide you in formulating an appropriate topic for the history of this sport?

If you have thought about a significant problem that existed in the sport or has continued to exist, you could develop a hypothesis question concerning that problem. For example: In the history of the game, what affect did audience behavior have on a minority player's performance in a given game, series of games, a season, or longer period of time? In this example, you have been given the behavior of the audience. In scientific terms, the given is the "independent variable." Given the behavior of the audience, how did it affect or influence the player's performance? Did the player improve or worsen or remain the same in performance? You want to observe how dependent the player's performance was on the behavior of the audience. For that hypothesis you identify performance as the "dependent variable." In an opposite case, you may be interested in the hypothesis question: What affect did the performance of the minority player have on audience reaction? In this new hypothesis, the given or "independent variable" is the player's performance. The "dependent variable" is audience reaction. In historical terms, did the audience change its behavior during a series of games, or a season? Why did it change? To what extent did it change? How did it change? In the two examples above we convert the hypothesis questions into the following statements of hypothesis. The affect (influence, impact) of audience behavior on player performance and the affect (influence, impact) of player performance on audience behavior.

If you do not recognize a problem leading to a hypothesis, you may want to explore a different methodology. Perhaps, you could join a men's or women's baseball team. You could become directly involved in the management of the team. Ask for permission to participate in the game or in some way observe management style and behavior. Through direct involvement in the sport, you become a participant observer. "Participant Observation Methodology" allows you to become an active member of the baseball community. It also allows you to examine directly, the "dynamics" or working of the game and the daily interaction among members of the team and management. By playing and/or observing the game you may find a historical topic to investigate. Perhaps, it could be the size of older stadiums or playing fields and their affects on performance. It could be changes in the structure or rules of the game as opposed to the way it was played in the past. What problems became apparent as the sport developed, and to what extent have changes solved those problems or left them unsolved? Whatever the case, participant observation methodology encourages you to take an active part in the history of the sport.

Suppose you choose not to join a team and not to become involved directly with management. If you are still interested in participant observation you could become a non-participant observer. "Non-participant Observation Methodology" allows you to immerse yourself in any and all aspects of the sport. However, you are not directly involved. You remain on the "side lines" so to speak. Analyze the evidence you need to gain insight into changes in the structure of the game and management of the team through time. At the same time you may study teams and management in other localities within the United States and observe the dynamics of the game and unsolved problems. Furthermore, you could study the same historical aspects as they apply to teams and management in other countries besides the United States. By interviewing team members as well as management, you may be able to learn how these changes affected the players' skills, records of achievement, and self-esteem (self-worth). Management may reveal the difficulties that owners and promoters have had with both the team and the general public. These difficulties may be part of the history of the sport and may have reoccurred in recent times.

In reference to "Survey Methodology," which will be discussed in the chapter, "*Statistics*," consider the design of questionnaires to be handed out or mailed to ball players, managers, and others involved in the sport. Depending upon answers, you could request a follow-up interview relating to a specific topic. On the other hand, you may prefer an "open-ended" discussion in which you have no prearranged questions to ask. In that case, you may want to construct questions for an additional interview after you have analyzed statements made during the open-ended interaction. It is common to ask for additional interviews after you have studied the answers to prior questions. Your follow-up questions may be very specific depending on the topic you finally select. Be sure to bring a tape recorder (with the interviewee's permission) so that you may focus on the direction of the interview and the responses given instead of trying to remember or write them, and trying to listen to the interviewee at the same time.

Another methodology you should explore and one you may enjoy studying is "Oral History Methodology." In oral history, you rely on audio/visual sources that have been stored in players' homes, in management offices, in private, public and school library collections as well as on the World Wide Web. By listening to voices of the past and seeing those who were directly or indirectly involved in baseball and its history, you may discover a problem that developed and remains unsolved. Perhaps, those voices may lead to unexplored social, political, or economic problems associated with the sport.

Consider "Case Study Methodology" which enables you to study a particular player, manager, or team in any locality of your choice. In case study, you are studying the dynamics of team interaction or the personality of an individual, as an example of the baseball community. Having interviewed team members, management personnel, listened to tapes and audio/visual sources, having examined library and online literature, why not choose a particular person, team, year, season to follow as completely as possible? Become totally immersed in the routine of the individual or team. What social, cultural, psychological, political, or economic pressures have surfaced as a result of case study?

If you like detective work, why not consider "Content Analysis Methodology"? For example, in content analysis, you may investigate, on a comparative basis, what was said, heard, and seen during a particular game by those who either watched the game or heard about it from others. By comparing the "content" of each source of information, you may be able to identify historical problems or events covered in one source and not in another or covered in several but varying in quantity of disclosed information and intensity of coverage. Content analysis methodology demands that you examine and compare an action, thought, or event identified in your sources. What is repeated? What is in agreement, disagreement? What is ignored? What is given little attention? You may find that one source furnishes you with information for a topic. However, a content analysis of the remaining sources reveals absence of the information you seek. Do not give up. Other methodologies may fill in the void.

In a subsequent chapter, interrogatives such as: what, when, where, how, why, who and whom will be introduced as avenues of historical inquiry. These interrogatives may raise researchable questions regarding baseball history. In the larger picture, they reflect a methodology referred to as "Descriptive Methodology." Descriptive methodology gives you opportunity to describe an event, incident, social interaction, or personality according to the question you have raised. These questions may originate from participant or non-participant observation, questionnaires, interviews, oral history, case study research, content analysis of library as well as online internet sources of information. Notice the following: What were the reactions of teammates to the inclusion of a new teammate of a different religion, or skin color? When did their reactions change? How? Why? For an example of a historical paper employing descriptive methodology, see the paper I wrote entitled, "When and Where was the First Public High School Established in the State of New York?" at the end of Chapter Fifteen.

In concluding, I offer three remarks. First, a literature search of the topic you have selected, in this case the history of baseball, may reveal that a study has already been done on your chosen hypothesis or descriptive question. In that case, it makes no sense to duplicate the study and the findings of another investigator. However, if your research reveals new evidence or refutes the findings of someone whose study you have examined, then it is absolutely necessary for you to disclose the new evidence in your own study. In addition, if you find that another investigator has examined a particular team or individual in one locality at a certain time in the history of baseball, you have the right to examine another individual or team in a different locality and, perhaps, different period of time. In that case, you are not copying nor plagiarizing another investigator's work.

Second, feel free to move from one methodology to another in pursuit of a problem or researchable question. Incorporate any and all methodologies into your writing from scientific to descriptive methodology. The flow from one to another gives you a greater range of inquiry that should hold your attention and at the same time provide expanded coverage of ways to investigate a topic.

Third, whatever methodology you choose in your quest for sources of information, employ the first process of history, "historical search" and/or "historical research." If, in looking for evidence about your selected topic, you discover a source that had not been previously known nor noted, you have initiated a "historical search." However, if in gathering additional evidence, you find information that had previously been discovered you have "re-searched" the source. That is, you are not the first person to discover that additional information. In the following two chapters, "The Primary Source" and "The Secondary Source," both pillars of historical search/research will be discussed.

# CHAPTER VI

## THE PRIMARY SOURCE

Have you ever considered yourself a "primary" or "first-hand" source? You, I, and every other person in this world are the most important primary sources in our individual life histories. What makes us primary? Whatever we think, say, believe, write or do is directly related to our life records. Of course, there are all the people who come in contact with you and me: our doctors, teachers, friends, families, and even our adversaries. They too, are primary sources. We also call them "eye and ear witnesses" because they see and/or hear us.

You may ask, "Why should anyone want to write about us?" The historian has written about people ever since human beings first learned to write their thoughts for others to read. It is not enough just to interview us in order to write a complete story of our lives. The writer should contact all those who see us, hear us, and talk with us. If the story is about you, then all those people who come in direct contact with you are primary sources in your history. When the historian interviews these people, he or she is relying on the spoken word. The investigator is not always so fortunate to contact eye and ear witnesses and speak with them directly. In your case, perhaps, some of your friends and relatives may no longer be available for comment. Will the historian give up? If the scholar had given up in the past, we would not know much about the ancient Greeks nor medieval civilization. Two hundred years from now will a historian be able to write about our civilization? Not one of us will be alive to give direct interviews. The historian will have to rely on evidence handed down to our children and to their children. He or she will examine what has been saved and preserved.

Where does the writer of history locate material for history? He or she may have to travel to find a witness, but generally learns to make use of primary evidence that is available. If the writer is studying your life, what may be available is a small percentage of your entire life story. This percentage may not include direct or "first-hand" interviews with eyewitnesses. However, there may be other kinds of primary source material about you. The form of written expression varies. It may be a letter written by you, or by someone who knows you and is discussing something one saw you do or heard you say. It may be a diary entry or a handful of notes written by some eyewitness. Scraps of paper containing messages about you may be found. Even an article written about you in a school newspaper by one of your friends is a primary source.

So far, we have been studying eye and ear witness accounts. There is a second type of primary source that may be useful to the study of your life history. It is "physical remains." If one wants to study some part of your life, it may be necessary to obtain information about your home, your favorite objects, and personal possessions. These artifacts are only a few examples of physical remains. What is the design of the neighborhood or the particular street on which you live? What does your home look like? How do you keep your possessions? Could the historian examine your neighborhood? It may not be possible. Neighborhoods change; your home may no longer be standing. To the professional, the structure of your home, your neighborhood, the size, shape, and condition of the possessions you value are all important in the study of physical remains. They all shed light on your history. Even what you look like, your physical appearance helps in rounding out an understanding not only of your personality but of your environment or home life.

A third type of primary source is the photograph. How simple it is in our modern age of digital photography to capture your neighborhood, your home, and your personal possessions in a picture. Everything from snapshots to movie film is primary as long as it captures you or some portion of your life activity. This evidence is just as important as eye and ear witness accounts in building a well-rounded picture of your life and personality. However, photographs may fade. They may be destroyed, lost, or given away. The problem of loss or destruction of pictures will be examined in the chapter on historical criticism.

A fourth type of primary source is a recording of your voice or a recording of an interview with you or with someone who knows you.  Your friends may have recorded some conversation you had with them. When talks or discussion panels are taped, these tapes may be preserved. In recent years, historians have begun to make collections of tapes, especially for oral history projects.

The written word, the interview, the physical remains, the photograph, or the recording do not complete the survey of primary source material available about you. A fifth type, artistic expression, may fill in the gaps and may therefore be of great value. Any kind of art work is primary material if the artist is an eyewitness to some event in your life. The sketch, drawing, or painting of you, of your home, neighborhood, or school life gives further evidence of your life experiences.

There remains one more type of primary or first-hand source: official documents. Records of your school, club, and your religious affiliation, or birth and marriage certificates, deeds, even the minutes of your club meetings are a limited number of all the possible official records covering your life. They have been written by someone in the organization and stamped with an official seal or signed by an officer of the organization to which you belong.

At this point the historian feels very much like a detective. He or she has been searching for and gathering primary evidence about your life. Now, we may realize how valuable primary materials are to the study of your life or any other person's life, but the work of the historian is not finished. The writer of history must study these materials very carefully. This part of the scholar's work will be discussed later.

# FOR FURTHER STUDY

The search for primary source material is never ending. Do you see why? What makes the search so difficult?

What connection do the words <u>search</u> and <u>research</u> have to the study of history?

How may you compare history writing to detective, crime, or mystery writing?

On the next page appears a letter by Eleanor Flexner, author of the book, <u>Century of Struggle: The Women's Rights Movement in the United States,</u> published by Harvard University Press in 1959. Miss Bressler, a former student, had decided to write to Miss Flexner for help in obtaining first-hand information. Miss Flexner sent the following reply:

January 14, 1964

Dear Miss Bressler:

Thank you very much for your kind words about my
book, "Century of Struggle". When I wrote it, I
hoped that school and college students would find it
helpful, and I am so glad that has been true of
you.

With regard to helping you in the matter of primary
sorces I ~~bsserks~~ am however afraid that I cannot
do much. For one thing the people who actually took
part in the closing years of the sugfrage campaign
have either died, or are very elderly indeed and
their memories are not very good. I really used everything I got from such people in the book and so
I do not think you would find much that was new by
talking to whatever survivors there still are.

Both newspapers and documentary material, such as
letters, rate as primary source material among historians, however, and here you might be more successful. If you live anywhere near Trenton, why don't
you write the State Archives there and ask whether
they have any material relating to the suffrage campaigns in New Jersey. They might have the papers of
the New Jersey suffrage organizations, or of individual
suffrage leaders.  If you will look in Volume V
of the History of Woman Suffrage (available in most
large college or city libraries) you will find on
pp. 412-433 a brief history of the sugfrage
movement in New Jersey, giving the names of
individual women who were active leaders--anyone
of these might lead you to private papers not yet
explored by any historian. Another good source are
back newspaper files, for papers in such cities as
Trenton and Newark.

Good luck to you!

With best wishes,

Sincerely yours,

*Eleanor Flexner*

By permission of Susan Bressler Eckstein and Eleanor Flexner

The above letter was photographed from the original and then reproduced.    No
changes have been made in structure, spelling, nor in punctuation.

# CHAPTER VII

## THE SECONDARY SOURCE

Is the "secondary" source of importance to your life history? Should the historian bother with secondary material when he or she feels that there is enough primary evidence available? The answers to these questions come when we examine the basic differences between primary and secondary sources. Even if there are sufficient eyewitness accounts about you, the historian still wants to gain as complete an understanding of your environment as possible. For example, the historian may want to interview other people in your town or in other towns similar in character and setting to yours.

"Why," you may ask, "take the round about way to get to the point?" The answer is simply that it is not enough to examine first-hand accounts that directly pertain to you. Indirectly, the people you seldom meet or see in town have an affect on you. They may set the clothing styles you like to wear. They may influence the school to make changes that affect the course of study you follow. They may give your town a certain type of reputation: a quiet town, a disorderly town. As long as you live in the same environment, you are a member of that community. Are you typical of the people in your neighborhood? In what ways are you typical? It should be clear to you that the secondary or second hand source has no direct contact with you. The interview with a person who has not met you is secondary material. The historian has interviewed that person not to know more about you, but to know more about your age group. What does it think? How does it act? How does it behave in public, in private? Are you typical of your peers?

The historian will not want to ignore any books that have been written on the subject of young people today. The writer of history may find that secondary sources are available with special references to life in towns, cities, or farming communities. Again, none of these books have been written about you in particular. There are no primary sources in them about your life. However, they do contain valuable information about your generation. They may contain references to interviews with religious leaders, club officials, school and law officials, or parents. Novels, plays, or short stories are also very helpful. All of these materials shed light on you as a member of society.

Consider why all of those interviews mentioned in this chapter are not primary source material for the study of your life history. The primary source makes reference to you directly. The secondary source has not had direct contact with you. Five hundred years from now a historian may want to write some additional history of your generation. The writer will be classified a secondary source because he or she will not have met you while you were alive. The scholar will only know you, as we say, "second hand." That is, the writer will have read what others have said about you. Perhaps, he or she will have read some secondary sources which will have been preserved and made available to read.

Suppose, in one of your letters you mention a special fountain pen or ballpoint pen you received as a present, but it cannot be found. Is there any value in examining other pens that are available in your town or community? Although these physical remains are substitutes, as secondary sources they are still valuable to the historian. Do you understand why? After all, they are not from your own collection. They are not primary. Yet, what do they show about our technology, about "American know-how"? As for your home, or neighborhood, if your particular house is no longer standing, other houses may be architecturally similar to yours. To the historian, what may be a typical home is very important to the study of your community life.

Do you still have any old photographs? Maybe, you are not interested in keeping pictures. Is there any point in trying to obtain secondary sources if they are photographs of other neighborhoods, of stores in which you do not shop, of people from another part of town? As in previous examples, these photographs are secondary because they do not pertain directly to you. We must keep in mind that they may be the only photographs of your community available many years from now.

The same holds true of official documents, artistic expressions, tapes of interviews, panels, discussions, and gatherings. All of these sources pertain to other people's lives. Not a single recording, drawing, sketch, nor official record may be available about you. However, each of these sources of information helps to increase our knowledge of you as a member of society. As for how typical you are of your age group, that subject will be investigated.

Before closing, I should like to explain that those people who know you and are primary sources in your life history, are secondary sources if they were not present at an event in which you participated or observed. They heard (hear say) about your participation or experience. If asked, they should explain that they heard about you from eye and ear witnesses or from secondary sources. Their accounts are then considered hear say. It may be necessary for the historical investigator to demonstrate, by examining their testimonies, that they were not credible (believable) eye and ear witnesses. Establishing credibility of a source of information as well as drawing conclusions will be discussed in the following two chapters, *Historical Criticism*" and "*Reaching Conclusions*." Both subjects are the pillars of the second process of history, "historical method."

## FOR FURTHER STUDY

Under what conditions may "primary evidence" be labeled, "secondary evidence"?

Is a secondary source admissable as evidence in a court of law? Why? Why not?

Egyptian Reproduction bust, XVIII Dynasty from Tell el Amarna. Head from statue of
Queen Nefertiti, Queen of King Akhenaten. Plaster cast of a painted limestone original
in Berlin. Bust of Nefertiti (thought to be 19th c. copy of sculptor in the Egyptian
Museum, Berlin). Museo Archeologico, Florence, Italy. Photo credit: Scala/Art Resource,
NY. A Secondary Source.

# CHAPTER VIII

## HISTORICAL CRITICISM

How many times have you read a section of a textbook and copied, word for word, the answer to some homework assignment? Have you ever stopped to notice the author's choice of words, style, or scholarship? You may say that since he or she is the author of the text recommended by your history department that automatically makes the scholar an authority on the subject of history. The author may have spent years studying primary and secondary sources for each chapter. However, no person is an authority on all of history.

Now, suppose the question is about your generation. You are reading a chapter from an assigned history text about life in the United States. You come across a few paragraphs devoted to young people of today. What is your opinion of the author? Do you still feel that the writer is an authority on the subject? How does the author treat you in general? Is the scholar sympathetic, indifferent, or even hostile to your age group? Is the historian fair? What does the scholar consider typical or atypical? Do you still feel that he or she has all the answers or would you like to compare the scholar's ideas with those of other writers?

Once we become involved in the investigation of an author's statements, ideas, and source material, we automatically become involved in the whole process of historical criticism. The professional historian, and you, the student of history, are both involved in the process of finding answers through investigation. It is important to read not only the assigned text but additional primary and secondary sources. Not taking for granted what a writer states without examination of what has been stated is the essence of critical thinking, a necessary part of historical criticism.

What happens when you compare your textbook to several others? One writer may emphasize a certain point while another either omits it or dismisses it as unimportant. Some writers include primary source material while others ignore such evidence. An author may actually state that contemporaries agree or disagree with the author's statements.

Would you say that it is important to know something about the background of the author? Is the author young? Is the writer one whose memories are fading? Is he or she a native of your country or a foreigner? Is he or she from the city, the countryside, or the suburbs? It may even help to know something about the historian's personality. If the scholar has lived a happy or miserable life, he or she may try to color the truth by distorting evidence. A writer who may be writing about you may choose to cite those primary sources that reveal the worst or best in you. This is distortion. It is also a case of historical prejudice or bias.

Again, this is exactly why you should not stop with one writer's opinion, view, or sources of information. You need to consider the nature of the primary sources included in the chapter. Are they delinquents, class presidents, or people from low, middle, or upper income families? Does the historian present various types of people? Does he or she try to paint a picture of the typical young American as only one kind of person?

Next, consider how the author constructs the chapter or the few paragraphs pertaining to your generation. Very often, you will find that the textbook writer will not cite primary source material, will not footnote his or her information, will not express his or her own doubts, and will not admit to ignorance about any point in the chapter. You may believe that as a writer of a textbook, he or she does not have to do all the above. Is your belief a defense for the writer who is introducing the topic to the student? Whatever the answer, it is necessary for you to investigate the subject matter.

Now, let us examine a historian's book on the subject of life in the United States. Let us examine a chapter on suburban or city living. How careful is the scholar? How much of a detective is he or she in writing? How much historical investigation and criticism does the historian offer of the evidence cited? It is very important for a writer to show somewhere the origin of the material used or quoted in the chapter. The sources referred to at the bottom of the page, the end of the chapter, or the end of the book tell something about the type of collected information. Would you stop to look at a footnote? You probably would if that footnote mentioned your name.

Suppose you have had interviews with the historian. In one case, the author has cited portions of your interview in a footnote. You read over what the author says you said. But look! The author is not telling the truth! You never said these things. Someone else must have given the writer this information. The footnote should have given credit to another person. Either that or maybe the author made up the interview. In another case, you come across something you said during an interview and you are angry with the printed version. The author has quoted only certain statements you made and purposely omitted others. "Why is the writer printing half the story?" you ask.

In the examples above, you have experienced two different kinds of reactions: "external" and "internal." In the first example you have discovered that the author used your name in the footnote and you know that you never gave evidence of any kind to this author. By external investigation, you have found an innocent mistake or a premeditated lie. It is not an authentic primary source since the interview cannot be credited to you. It could be that the interview was with another person and that the author has confused you with that individual. Someone will have to correct this external error.

In the second case, although it has been established externally that you did give the interview, internal criticism reveals that the author has changed the meaning you want to convey. Whoever reads that book will understand only part of your feelings. The rest will be hidden from the world unless someone takes the time and effort to examine the interview to see exactly what you did say. This is the time when the investigator must review the quoted material to see if the complete version or just a portion of it is being given.

To examine more closely what is meant by internal investigation, let us return to the interview that took place between you and the author. Let us suppose that during the original interview the author asked how you feel about parents. You answer, "Parents are stupid because they are afraid to say 'No' to us." But what you read in the final version is the following: "Parents are stupid because they are afraid...." The extra dots indicate that the author has purposely left out some of your statement. Will the reader go to the bother of reading your complete statement? In the portion above, one may have the impression that you think parents are stupid and cowardly. However, you may actually sympathize with parents. You may want to show that you understand them and their possible need to be your pal, or do you feel that parents have a need to be your pal? Is this thought something that the investigator has interpreted from you remark? If so, then you have additional problems of internal criticism. An author may intentionally, or unintentionally, exaggerate, distort, or understate your thoughts. The writer may absorb what he or she wishes to hear, wants to believe, or already believes. In sum, internal criticism considers the psychology of human emotions and feelings which lie beneath the surface of human thoughts and actions.

Any kind of visual or illustrative materials included in the chapter must also be examined critically. These materials present their own special problems of external and internal evaluation. Let us suppose that there is a sketch of some clothing. Could it be proven externally that this style is worn by people of your age? Is there another type of primary source that corroborates this sketch? Perhaps, there is a letter written by one of your peers that describes a new style of clothing that he or she has worn. The answer could help clear up the external problem. What if only middle-aged people are seen wearing this type of clothing? Also, simply the fact that models may pose for clothing advertisements does not mean that the youth of today wear that certain style. Does the illustration used in the chapter represent what manufacturers would like to sell rather than what they actually have sold? Each of these questions relates to the external matter of establishing how authentic the source is.

If the style of clothing is proven to be worn by your age group, one may ask, "What do the people think of the style? How do they feel when they wear it?" These questions are the domain of internal investigation and criticism. Although it may be proven that a certain number of you wear this clothing style, the historian may exaggerate the need you have for this kind of clothing. The author may purposely underestimate its importance to you. For example, how often do you wear the particular style, on what occasions, and to what places?

Instead of a sketch, the author may select a photograph for the chapter. He or she may choose a reprint of some old or very faded photograph. If a color picture is faded, it may suggest that this particular style is rather shabby looking, or "washed out," and that, perhaps, only the poorest people would wear these clothes. Dust embedded in the original photograph may also give the impression of worn out or dirty clothes in the reprint. The historian may select a photograph that shows a model posing in front of a clothing store in a very exclusive part of town. One may believe that this style is worn by more wealthy students. In such cases, externally it has been proven that the photographs have been taken in your town; that the clothes worn by the models are authentic. Internal investigation reveals that both pictures distort the perception and feelings the reader has of the photographs.

Not only faded, but under and overexposed photographs may completely change the character of the subject. A picture of your house or neighborhood may have an entirely different appearance in an underdeveloped, color photograph. It may make one imagine that you live in a very sunny area, when actually the neighborhood receives little or no sunshine because of the surrounding high buildings. Angle shots present additional internal problems and may confuse us when we compare these photographs with written accounts of your neighborhood.

For example, we find a primary source that describes your town as a quiet, residential community in the suburbs. Yet, the photograph selected for the chapter was taken during a local parade in which the town seemed overcrowded. The view does not support the primary account. The picture has been taken in such a way that the people do not look as if they are marching in the middle of the street but appear to be walking on the sidewalks. A view like this destroys the internal worth of the source.

An even greater oversight in internal evaluation occurs when an author finds a photograph of some person you know, and the historian does not realize that the original photograph was touched up in some way. In developing the picture, the photographer could have deleted or changed any unattractive features. You will be able to notice something wrong when you find other photographs with which to compare the one selected by the writer. Why has the writer selected that particular photograph?

Suppose there should be a fire started by a vandal in your neighborhood and someone photographs it. By coming very close to the fire, the photographer may exaggerate its intensity. Actually, there was a small fire on the first floor of someone's house, and the fire was kept under control. Only one portion of a room was damaged. Externally, the photograph is valid because it does show at least that one room. If the historian is prejudiced against you or your town, he or she may even choose this picture in order to prove that your community is not safe from vandalism. The scene could have a negative effect on the reader and could cause many well-meaning Americans to look down upon your generation's behavior. Internal criticism has uncovered a distortion of truth.

The artist whose work is reproduced in the chapter may or may not have observed first-hand the scene he or she has sketched or painted. The artist could have painted from memory or could have made on-the-spot sketches. It is absolutely necessary to try to discover externally if the artist was a witness to or a participant in the event which has taken place. Many artists are given assignments in which they are paid to illustrate some aspect of history. Their drawings may be completely secondary material. Yet, the reader who is not acquainted with historical criticism or historical analysis may believe that the artist was there at the time of the happening. In your case, the artist may have never seen you, your friends, nor your neighborhood, but has attempted to make a drawing based on a primary or secondary account.

How the artist portrays the individual or scene is a fascinating aspect of external and internal evaluation. The final artistic work will depend not only on how skilled the artist is, or on what art education he or she received, but also on one's entire life experience. The artist may not draw you as you appear to your family, your friends, or to you, but according to what you look like to him or her. If the artist has lived in the city, and dislikes living in the suburbs, he or she may even try to paint a negative picture of your home town. By the use of drab colors, the artist may distort the attractiveness of the community. What may a second artist do with the same scene? The finished canvas may turn out to be the opposite of the first scene. Which canvas will the historian select for the chapter? Will the historian have available more than one artist's version? The question of selectivity of materials will be more fully examined in Chapter X, "Historiography."

How may the artist paint your portrait? You are known to be a friendly, positive person. However, your portrait shows you as a moody, pensive individual. Is this your normal expression? Is it momentary? The artist may believe that your generation is too defiant. You may become the target of his or her attack; you appear as a tough person. The internal feelings of the artist are then revealed.

Examining the internal reliability of a source is one of the most absorbing and interesting tasks for the investigator. Should we rely on the testimony provided by eye and ear witnesses or secondary sources? What people have been quoted? Are they sympathetic or hostile to your age group? Are they the best choices of sources of information? Are they available to the historian? What makes them the best or the worst choices? Do they represent a wide range of opinions held by the population of today? Should the investigator rely on the spoken or written words, on the witnesses, on the drawings, or on the photographs?

Of writing which is autobiographical in nature: that is, written by someone about his or her own life experiences, the autobiography may have been written long after the event in which the writer participated. Exactly, when and where did the first writing or first interview take place? In your case, the chapter may contain an interview or some autobiographical notes you made at the age of twenty one. It is now a long time since you were young. How much have you forgotten? How much have you left out? Why? How much have you changed? Are you still in sympathy with the younger generation? You may now have a son or a daughter of your own. He or she may annoy you at times. How much have you purposely omitted from your interview and notes? These questions of internal reliability may take the investigator days, weeks, or months to examine and corroborate.

The chapter may contain printed extracts of a recording you made during your school days. Once proven to be externally credited to you, how reliable is the speech you made at an assembly? Did you mean what you said? Did you say those things to impress or annoy school officials? Did any of your original comments have to be censored? Was the original tape spliced or edited in some way? By whom and why? Does the writer weigh what you say? Are the remarks you made typical of your age group? Has the writer bothered to corroborate your statements with those of other witnesses?

Official records used in the chapter are ready for internal inspection once they have been analyzed for external authenticity and/or forgery. Examining for possible forgery requires, for example, that the ink used in the writing must be studied to see if that ink was in use at the time the official record was dated. Does the paper on which it was written or typed represent the type of paper in use during the time period in question? Handwriting experts may have to verify a particular style of handwriting. Also, a chemist may have to assist the historian. External inspections go on with other kinds of primary sources. Verification must be made regarding the following: photography equipment and paper for photographs, art paper and artistic equipment, and chemical content of all types of physical remains. Of course, there are limits to the facilities and equipment people have available to them to establish such verification.

How internally reliable is that official record? At a meeting you attended, a recording secretary took the official notes for the organization. Perhaps, the minutes were altered. Maybe, the secretary changed the intent of some of the statements you and your friends made at the meeting. Perhaps, the secretary disliked a particular remark that was made and omitted it from the final draft. The secretary's bias or prejudice, and even his or her personality may have interfered with much of the value of the official primary source, and may have destroyed its value. However, there may have been someone who was sitting in the back row who took down every remark that was made that evening (a newspaper reporter?). That primary source is not official because it was written by someone other than the delegated secretary of the organization. Will the historian search for any other available accounts of the meeting? Will he or she compare other accounts with the official recording?

Unfortunately, writers borrow material from each other. When they do this without evaluating the material, they may pass onto the public the same lies, distortions, and exaggerations that become folklore. Would you be annoyed to see the same statement made about your generation by several writers? Would you wonder why they did not discuss each other's source material or point of view? Would you wonder why each has not tried to obtain new evidence?

No discussion of historical criticism is complete without reference to the author's style of writing. Language, choice of words, and sense of humor all have a bearing on the final outcome of the work. Does the author use the vocabulary of today? Is the author fluent in the latest expressions? Does he or she bring out views in an interesting and informative manner? Does he or she make a point clearly? Does the author make liberal or sparse use of examples and illustrations? Does the writer admit to ignorance or lack of sufficient evidence? Does the author come to any definite conclusions?

In the following chapter you will see how the historian draws conclusions from the knowledge gained through historical evaluation and criticism. After analyzing all sources, the author's task is to put together and reconstruct the past as carefully and (we hope) as objectively as possible.

# FOR FURTHER STUDY

Turn to the chapter on the American Revolution in a textbook. Read the section on the Battle of Lexington. Compare this section with at least two additional sources. Perhaps, you may find a textbook dated many years ago. Do the texts state who fired the first shot on Lexington Green? Which author seems to you to be more reliable? Why?

In the year 1770, the Boston Massacre occurred. How many people were actually "massacred"? Who were the victims?

Try to obtain reprints of portraits of George Washington. Do the various artists paint the same features of the first President? Which portrait of Washington do you think is the most accurate? Why?

If we read the translated versions of the history of World War II recorded by historians from countries on opposite sides of the war, do you think that their versions would agree? Why? Why not?

Try to obtain photographs of Abraham Lincoln between the years 1861 and 1865. Which is the best likeness of Lincoln? Why?

When you are in the library, examine the collection of works on the history of art. Also, look at references which list artist by name, date of birth, and nationality.

Photo courtesy of the Library of Congress.
Battle of Lexington, engraved by Hammatt Billings.

Did Billings paint the above picture at the time of the American Revolution?  Was he an eyewitness?  How may you find the answers to the questions?

Photo courtesy of the Library of Congress. Battle of Lexington, painted by Bicknell.

Do the patriots seem more aggressive in this version? Which of the two versions would you include in a history of the American Revolution? Why?

# CHAPTER IX

## REACHING CONCLUSIONS

By now you are able to identify and analyze both primary and secondary sources. You have learned how to examine each type for external authenticity and internal reliability. You have, no doubt, begun to realize the importance of examining an author's choice of language, readability, imaginativeness, scholarship, and use of documented sources. You are also bound to notice if the writer questions his or her own thinking, findings, or the evidence of other scholars. You may notice if the writer admits ignorance or lack of sufficient evidence. Now, you are ready for the next step in the method of historical inquiry. Consider the conclusions the author draws for sections of the chapter. These conclusions are based on "fact" or "certainty," "probability," "possibility," and "uncertainty."

What does the historian mean by the terms "fact," or "certainty"? One tends to think of a fact as a statement that is "absolutely certain," true beyond any reasonable doubt. Often, people say, "I know for a fact that…." But the historian does not rely on such a statement made in conversation. He or she may be too polite to say so, but in the back of the mind run the questions, "How do you know for certain that….? Are you able to prove it?" For the professional investigator, "fact" means absolute reality as far as the historian has been able to determine. Naturally, the investigator has many problems to solve before approaching fact or certainty.

After intensive critical examination of hundreds of primary and secondary accounts, the historian may find that only a handful of these sources is externally authentic and internally reliable. When the historian discovers two or more independent and reliable primary sources which agree on a particular point in question, and all remaining secondary sources support the primary evidence, the historian may come to a conclusion of fact or certainty on that one point.

For example, your school is being studied and the question has surfaced as to how many floors the school building now has. The scholar has found three available independent and reliable primary sources which mention the height of the building. One of these is a recent photograph which clearly shows the two floors of the school. The second is an extract from an official record at the Board of Education which mentions the number of disabled students who have difficulty in reaching their second floor class at the top of the building. The third statement comes from the pen of a teacher who has requested a change of room assignment from the second floor to the first because the teacher is annoyed at having to climb the stairs to the top floor.

Why did I use the term, "independent" in the previous paragraph? Although all three of the above primary sources give the same testimony about the number of floors, each source is entirely unrelated to and independent of the others in either physical or social ways. The photograph stands as inanimate visual proof. The teacher has a separate function in the school and a more distinct relationship to it than does the Board of Education. The educator may be annoyed that he or she was given a room so far away from the main office. The Board of Education record on the above-mentioned students represents the public interest in the students and responsibility for their welfare. You realize, no doubt, why all of the above primary sources are considered independent. Otherwise, could it be proven that someone in the Board office collaborated with the teacher and made a complaint about the number of floors; that the teacher took the snapshot as proof of a complaint? You may begin to question the reliability of the testimony.

Examining secondary sources referred to by the author, you find that the author has relied on local histories of education or textbooks on the subject of school administration. All of these sources mention that the typical school has two floors. One of the writers has supported statements with an official report given by the State Department of Education. Another has footnoted references from local histories. Still, another author has cited letters received from Boards of Education in response to questions about the architecture of their schools. Several other writers offer no proof, nor do they cite any evidence, nor use any footnotes. However, they all agree that the typical school contains two floors. Interestingly, during the evaluation of evidence, an investigator notices that a particular secondary source completely differs from the others. The author of that one study states that the typical school has only one floor. The author may have done insufficient research to support that conclusion, or may have relied on some prejudiced accounts and, perhaps, could have missed other important primary material. If the work of that writer is evaluated as inferior in quality and scholarship, the conclusion of certainty of two floors remains.

Frequently, in the field of history, one finds that new writers may come to rely on the judgments and conclusions of well known and highly renowned authorities. These people may either purposely or subconsciously accept or perpetuate earlier findings. By blind acceptance, the scholar is actually adding weight to earlier conclusions and is helping to strengthen them. But the modern investigator must be on the lookout for this kind of imitation. The historian should try to probe as deeply as possible into the work of earlier historians to see how carefully they drew their conclusions.

The word "probability" suggests an entirely different conclusion to the trained scholar. When an individual says to you that it "probably will rain," you have the feeling that it most likely will rain. However, you are not positive. Nor is the person who forecasts the weather. The historian uses the term, "probability," in a similar way. If the historian is not certain about an answer to a historical question or problem, he or she obviously should not come to a conclusion of absolute fact. What makes the historian almost positive? The investigator has discovered one primary source which has stood the tests of external and internal criticism. Many secondary sources support the evidence revealed by that one primary source.

Return to the problem concerning the number of floors in your local school. In the new case, only one primary source has been proven authentic and reliable. It is the photograph of the building. We also have information in secondary sources that states that the typical number of floors is two. The photograph clearly shows second floor staircases and second floor windows. The historian will, therefore, conclude that it is probable that your school has two floors.

"Probability" to the historian means only one primary source supported by a sufficient number of reliable secondary sources. There is no set number of secondary works needed. At least two independent and competent secondary writers should support the testimony of one first-hand source. By using the word, "independent," we hope that these authors have not relied on the conclusions of each other. We also hope that as few as possible cultural, regional, or group prejudices have affected their conclusions.

For example, one may strongly suspect some prejudiced thought and judgment from the findings of two modern scholars who have both graduated from suburban schools. Each may come to the conclusion that the typical American school has two floors. Perhaps, these investigators have had little or no contact with city schools. Many city schools have more than two stories. These scholars may have strong prejudices against city people and, therefore, against city institutions. They may have overlooked the importance of the city school.

Have you ever heard the comment, "Anything is possible"? By the term, "possibility," we mean that there is no primary source available to the scholar. The investigator may have examined many first-hand accounts and found each one to be either externally or internally worthless. All that remain are secondary sources which basically give the same information. How may one come to the conclusion of possibility concerning your school?

Suppose that five hundred years from now, some scholars will be investigating the type of education your generation received. It will be important to know how large a school population existed and how adequate the facilities of the schools were. Will there be any primary sources available for them to analyze? The aging of photographs may completely destroy their future value. Student records may have to be burned for lack of sufficient space in which to store them. Fire may destroy the Board of Education office records. The school itself, a physical holdover, may completely change. Floors may be added. The building may be torn down and replaced by an entirely different type of structure. No present day eyewitness will be living to tell the story of the building's construction. What will professional historians do?

They will be fortunate to find written secondary accounts of the history of education. Two of these histories may contain some statements about the two floors that once existed. Historians, then, may write that, perhaps, there were two floors in schools during the year 200_. If no other authors dispute this statement, the conclusion of possibility will be reached. Unless a conscious effort is made to preserve that information which you and all of us possess about society, scholars will be writing about the possibilities of our way of life and experiences. Our future offspring will not be sure about everyday things we see, take for granted, and know for certain exist today.

One of the most absorbing and interesting aspects related to the establishment of conclusions is the problem of using copied primary source materials. If original accounts have been destroyed by time, fires, etc., extracts or excerpts of them may still appear in various secondary sources. The operations of external and internal evaluation will naturally determine the usefulness of these extracts. These operations may, also, help us to reach unexpected conclusions. If the original primary sources have been lost or destroyed, how will the historian know that there were originals? If the author, whose work the investigator has been analyzing, has neglected to include footnotes indicating where he or she obtained the primary sources, the investigator will have to discount the quoted excerpts as inauthentic. In such a case, the conclusion of possibility will remain since we may not take quoted materials for granted without additional proof of authenticity.

In the case of a writer who claims to have examined primary material such as photographs of the scene he or she has been describing, should one trust the writer? Did the writer actually see the photographs? When future historians examine the writer's work, will they search for those photographs? Some scholars will believe the writer and will accept his or her discussion of photographic evidence. However, others will not accept the writer's statements. If the writer has neglected to include copies of photographs in the narrative, we have only the writer's word. One's word is not enough in the analysis of evidence.

The final conclusion, which is called "uncertainty," is, perhaps, the most difficult for the student and writer of history as well as for the general public to accept. We would like to have definite answers to the questions we raise. But in a world of uncertainties, such as we live in today, who may predict what will happen tomorrow? We may be uncertain about which way we should go, what course to pursue, what path to take. How does the professional historian use the word, "uncertainty"? The investigator reaches the conclusion of uncertainty when he or she finds some unanswerable conflict among the sources of information. The disagreements may occur between two or more primary sources, two or more secondary sources, or between at least one primary and one secondary source.

Returning once more to the question of number of floors in your local school, we now have discovered that the only official Board of Education record available states clearly that there are two floors. We find an equally reliable photograph that shows one floor. Obviously, one of these sources is incorrect. But which one? Both have been completely tested for external authenticity and internal reliability. Both have passed the tests of investigation. Until some further evidence is unearthed which could prove that one of these sources is wrong, we must conclude that the number of floors is either one or two. In other words, we are uncertain about that particular point.

It should not surprise you to observe that we do not all see, hear, nor remember the same things. You and your friends may witness an event and later discuss what happened. Does it seem odd that you may each state something different? You remember something that you said which other people do not recollect. They remember details which you do not recall. We may all witness the same event. Yet, no two accounts may completely agree.

As you review the material presented in this chapter, the operations establishing conclusions should become clear to you. Important are the type and number of authentic and reliable sources available at the time of investigation. Conclusions should be based upon <u>external</u> accuracy and authenticity as well as upon <u>internal</u> objectivity. Consequentially, what primary and/or secondary accounts are usable? As more evidence is discovered, earlier conclusions are either strengthened or weakened. New evidence may change facts to probabilities, possibilities, or uncertainties. You may question if historians will reach a point at which their conclusions will be unchangeable. In the field of historical methodology, unlike a court of law, the case is never closed. Searching and researching for evidence will continue as long as historians and the public are interested in studying historical topics. Conclusions are not irrevocable as long as scholars are willing to examine evidence.

Finally, it is most important to understand that fact and certainty are equivalent to reality to the historian who has reached these conclusions. Other scholars may regard the same evidence that was concluded to be fact as something less than certain. It is natural to have conflicting or differing conclusions since no writer in the field may expect everyone else to agree with all of his or her conclusions. This is why one must remain objective when one reviews the conclusions drawn by other scholars.

# FOR FURTHER STUDY

Have a group of people act out a skit or role play. At the same time, ask others to be official reporters for selected newspapers. Ask them to write what they saw and heard. One half of the reporters should take notes immediately. The other half should be asked to wait a few minutes. When the notes have all been written, ask the reporters to give their versions. Do they agree entirely? What are the areas of fact, probability, possibility, or uncertainty?

How does a jury establish the guilt or innocence of the accused?

In several foreign languages the subjunctive mood is used to express doubt or uncertainty. Why is the indicative mood used to express certainty? How are the words, "probably" and "possibly" used in romance languages; how are they used in other languages? For examples, translate the following four sentences into French or Spanish:

1) It is certain that John is coming home.
2) It is not certain that John is coming home.
3) It is probable that John is coming home.
4) It is possible that John is coming home.

The following paragraph appears in the work, Abraham Lincoln: The Prairie Years and the War Years, by Carl Sandburg, page 44. Notice how Mr. Sandburg uses such terms as "certain," "probably," and "possibly."

> During that year, of whatever letters he wrote only three were kept and saved and they were scant and perfunctory, shedding no light on his personal life or love or growth. It was certain that Ann Rutledge and Lincoln knew each other and he took interest in her; probably they formed some mutual attachment not made clear to the community; possibly they loved each other and her hand went into his long fingers whose bones told her of refuge and security. They were the only two persons who could tell what secret they shared, if any. It seemed definite that she had had letters from McNamar and probably after a time she had once written him that she expected release from her pledge. Summer of 1835 came and in September it would be three years since McNamar had gone, more than two years since any letter had come from him.

Photo courtesy of the Library of Congress

Abraham Lincoln in Urbana, Illinois, April 25, 1858. From a glass ambrotype by Samuel G. Alschuler. The above print and the two which follow show the uncertainties of physical characteristics.

Photo courtesy of the Library of Congress

A. Lincoln in Pittsfield, Illinois, October 1, 1858. Ambrotype by Calvin Jackson.

Photo courtesy of The Library of Congress.

A. Lincoln in Chicago, Illinois, October 4, 1859.  Photograph by Samuel M. Fassett.

**Matching Conclusions**

Y = Types of Conclusion

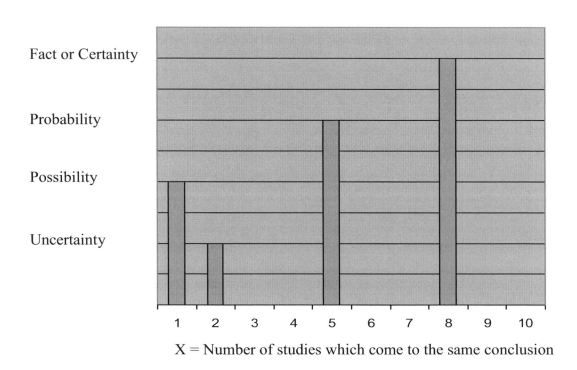

X = Number of studies which come to the same conclusion

If you are a history educator, assign the identical topic for a paper to more than one student. When the papers are completed compare the students' conclusions.

The Abraham Lincoln-Ann Rutledge Romance

Cathy Michalski
For
Jack Block
Fair Lawn High School
By permission of
Catherine Michalski Benvento

# INTRODUCTION

In 1831, twenty-two year old Abraham Lincoln, having recently started out on his own, took up residence in the Rutledge tavern of New Salem, Illinois. It was here in this small community that Lincoln first began his study of law. It was here, also, that he launched the political career that reached its climax in his election as the sixteenth President of the United States

Two years after his election to the presidency in 1860, there appeared in the small town newspaper, The Menard Axis of Petersburg, Illinois, an unflattering account of the Lincoln of thirty years before and of a romance he had with a young girl of New Salem.

The article was the beginning of one of the greatest legends in American history. While it became part of American folklore, it remained a center of historical controversy: The Abraham Lincoln-Ann Rutledge romance, fact or fiction?

This writer defines the word, "romance," as a love affair. No problem exists concerning this definition as the writer believes the term was used in 19th century America to mean the same as it does in 20st century America.

The article mentioned in the introduction was titled, "A Romance of Reality," and was written by a Mr. John Hill who published it on February 15, 1862. He describes Lincoln as an ungainly youth and lovelorn swain. As Benjamin Thomas relates in his biography of Lincoln, "…Hill told of how the awkward young man had met and wooed a young belle of the village and won her heart. They planned to be married but the maiden died, and her lover became so melancholy that friends feared he might attempt suicide…."[1]

This writer questions the qualifications of Hill as an objective witness to this episode. Hill was addressing an anti-Lincoln audience. His account was published thirty years after the supposed event and there were a few flaws in his narrative.[2] His memories were apparently indirect, for he later admitted that at that time of Lincoln's stay in New Salem, "I knew no more as to who he was then I did of the inhabitants of the Feegee Island."[3] He apparently obtained his information from his father, Samuel Hill, who had been a merchant of New Salem when Lincoln resided there. Hill had been postmaster for a time but had lost his job due to a charge of neglect, and Lincoln took over.[4] He also sought but lost the hand of Ann Rutledge, not to Lincoln but to a John McNamar. The question then arises: could the senior Hill, over the course of thirty years, have confused his disappointment over the loss of his postmaster's job which did involve Lincoln with his loss of Ann Rutledge in which Lincoln apparently was not involved? In any case, prejudice on the part of this witness must be considered.

Hill's article attracted little attention, but it did inspire William H. Herndon, a former law partner of Lincoln, to seek additional information.[5] As B. Thomas relates in his biography:

> "…he prepared a lecture delivered at Springfield, Illinois on November 16, 1866. From this the world first learned that Lincoln loved Ann Rutledge with 'all his soul, mind and strength,' that her love for him was equally strong, but that, finding herself engaged to Lincoln and McNamar at the same time and wishing to be perfectly honest with both, Ann became so torn in spirit that she could neither eat nor sleep. Racked with fever, she became weak….On August 25, 1835 Ann died."[6]

Herndon also included a touching account of Lincoln's visit to her sickroom, declaring "The meeting was quite as much as either could bear…." He perpetuated Hill's account of Lincoln's insanity after her death, and further declared that Lincoln to his death never loved any other woman.[7]

---

[1]Benjamin Thomas, <u>Abraham Lincoln, A Biography</u>, pp. 49-50.
[2]James G. Randall, <u>Mr. Lincoln</u>, p. 53.
[3]Ruth Randall, <u>Mary Lincoln: A Biography</u>, p. 403 as taken from John Hill to Herndon, Petersburg, Ill., June 27, 1865.
[4]William E. Barton, <u>The Life of Abraham Lincoln</u>, pp. 212-213.
[5]Thomas, <u>op. cit.</u>, p. 50.
[6]<u>Ibid.</u>, p. 50-51.
[7]<u>Ibid.</u>, p. 51.

Herndon is the world's main source of information concerning the Lincoln-Rutledge romance. Many subsequent biographies were based on his material, such as those written by Ward H. Laman,[8] and Ida M. Tarbell.[9] This writer has considered this when quoting these sources, for Herndon's credit as an accurate historian is questionable. His motives for writing his lecture, his methods of research, and the reliability of his witnesses bear careful scrutiny.

Both Benjamin Thomas and James Randall agree that Herndon obtained his material by interviewing old settlers and in some cases their children. If he could not personally interview them, he had them interviewed by proxy or got their statements by correspondence.[10]

All the statements collected by Herndon were efforts to recall what happened thirty years before. Ruth Randall in her criticism of Herndon even suggests they were obtained "...largely under his prodding or suggestion"[11] and that he used his skills as a lawyer to sway their thinking.[12] She uses this quote attributed to Herndon to help prove her point: "Men and women are inquisitive and hint a thing to them only and they will flesh the story falsely seen to suit the demands of the mind." [13] In all fairness, it must be mentioned that Herndon said this in another connection, not specifically about the Ann Rutledge case; but it does raise doubts as to his methods of research.

The above mentioned authors have all seriously doubted Herndon's theory; but it is interesting to note that even William E. Barton, a firm believer in the romance, questioned Herndon's reliability as a historian.[14] He states "... Herndon was a diligent if not always a discriminating gatherer of facts regarding Abraham Lincoln. When his book states a fact, within the range of his own observations, it is reliable.... But when he draws an inference, he is often wrong."[15] Both Randalls, James[16] and Ruth,[17] agree that Herndon had a tendency to psychoanalyze and to be sentimental, to which Barton agrees, calling him a man of "emotional temperament."[18] The Dictionary of American Biography states that Herndon did dramatize his materials.[19] This writer has found, by examining two of Herndon's letters, that he had a tendency to change his mind. In a letter dated February 25, 1870 and written to Ward Laman, Herndon states, "What I stated to Arnold (Issac Arnold who wrote a Life of Lincoln in 1885) was and is true. Mr. Lincoln loved Ann Rutledge to his death, no mistake."[20] However, in a letter dated August 22, 1887,

---

[8]Loc.cit.
[9]Ida Tarbell, In the Footsteps of the Lincolns, p. 213.
[10]J. Randall, op. cit., p. 55; B. Thomas, op. cit., p. 50.
[11]R.Randall, op.cit., p. 397
[12]Ibid., p. 396.
[13]Ibid., pp. 396-397, as taken from Herndon to Weik, Springfield, January 22, 1887.
[14]Barton, op. cit., p. 214.
[15]Ibid., p. 219.
[16]J.Randall, op. cit., p. 55.
[17]R. Randall, op. cit., p. 397.
[18]Barton, op. cit., p. 219.
[19]William H. Herndon Dictionary of American Biography, 1932, Vol. 8, p. 579.
[20]Emanuel Hertz, The Hidden Lincoln: From the Letters and Papers of William H. Herndon, p. 65.

Herndon, writing to a Mr. Bartlett states, "…the Anne Rutledge story, the facts of it, did affect Lincoln's life, I know up to '42 and it is quite LIKELY longer, POSSIBLY to his death".[21] (capitalization this writer's emphasis) It was such information, as stated in the first letter, upon which Laman based his biography. He apparently thought it was fact, and one can only wonder how many of his readers believed this also. Yet seventeen years later, by Herndon's own admission, it could not be considered fact.

What were Herndon's motives in exposing this romance? Ruth Randall states that Herndon was antagonistic to Mrs. Lincoln and believes "An early sweetheart for Lincoln would serve his purpose beautifully.[22] That Herndon and Mrs. Lincoln did not get along is a matter of public record; their exchange of open letters in newspapers testifies to that fact. But that Herndon published his lecture to antagonize Mrs. Lincoln, there is only the word of Miss Randall. It must be remembered that Miss Randall's book is an effort to bolster Mrs. Lincoln's public image, and Herndon was instrumental in lowering it originally.

Herndon himself stated in a letter dated August 22, 1887, "… if this nation wants great men, it must build up great women…."[23] Did Herndon just "build up" Ann Rutledge? Even as severe a critic as Ruth Randall feels he had to have some clue or shred of what he considered evidence before he started his search.

The Herndon-Weik Collection was made public in 1942. Those authors who have had access to the collection agree in their appraisal of it. B. Thomas[24] and R. Randall[25] agree it is a mass of contradictory evidence. David Donald states that the more people repeated their tales, the surer they became of them.[26]

It seems that those people who were closest to Lincoln and Ann knew least about any romance. Robert B. Rutledge, Ann's brother and one of Herndon's most important witnesses, wrote Herndon that he trusted in his "…honesty and integrity as a historian…" to go over his (Rutledge's) statements and correct them, indicating he thought Herndon was the authority on the subject and not himself.[27] The information Rutledge did supply was inconsistent. At one point he said Lincoln and Ann's engagement was "conditional" i.e., dependent upon release from McNamar; elsewhere he stated it was "not conditional but absolute."[28] Mentor Graham, who had taught both Lincoln and Ann, supported the tradition of the engagement.[29] Yet concerning seeing Lincoln as a boy in Kentucky in 1819 and 1820 he is badly mistaken, for the Lincolns moved to Indiana in 1811.[30] While this does not disprove the old schoolmaster's previous testimony, it raises doubts

---

[21]Ibid., p. 201.
[22]R. Randall, op. cit., p. 396.
[23]Hertz, op. cit., p. 201.
[24]Thomas, op. cit., p. 50.
[25]R. Randall, op. cit., p. 397.
[26]David Donald, Lincoln's Herndon, p. 187.
[27]R. Randall, op.cit., pp. 398-399, as taken from R.B. Rutledge to Herndon, October 22, and October 30, 1866, Herndon-Weik mss.
[28]J. Randall, op. cit., p. 59.
[29]Ibid., p. 56.
[30]Ibid., p. 57.

concerning the reliability of his memory. Ida Tarbell quotes a Mr. Henry Rankin as a secondary witness to the love affair. Miss Tarbell contends that Rankin's mother was Ann's confidant during the time of the supposed engagement. Mr. Rankin says that it was in the early summer of 1835 that Ann first confided to his mother that she had become engaged to Mr. Lincoln.[31] While the three witnesses quoted above were among those who recalled the romance, there are others equally competent who remembered nothing about it. R. J. Onstatt, a native of New Salem, declared concerning the romance, "...the Story is a lie out of Whole Cloth." John McNamar wrote "I never heard...(any) person say that Mr. Lincoln addressed Miss Ann Rutledge in terms of courtship...."[32]

While this writer has, up to this point, criticized Herndon and his witnesses, it now becomes necessary to evaluate the sources consulted by this writer. The biographies of Lincoln written by Thomas and Sandburg both include bibliographies indicating the authors' sources of information. This writer has found that both historians write in a critical and analyzing style. James Randall's work is especially noteworthy because of his extensive evaluation and criticism of information. This writer has found Ruth Randall's book to include extensive footnotes and bibliography. Aside from the previously mentioned possible prejudice, this writer finds her work invaluable when considering the romance. However, this writer is more critical of Ida Tarbell's book. Miss Tarbell has included neither footnotes nor bibliography. In addition, this writer has observed her style to be far too subjective and emotional. For example, she does not question Rankin's testimony but bases her belief in his reliability on the dignity and expression of Mr. Rankin. William Barton, while more critical in his analysis of material than Miss Tarbell, seems to be too emotional also. This writer has observed in his work a strong dislike of McNamar. Mr. Barton goes to great lengths to discredit McNamar and his prejudice must be considered when weighing his opinion included later in this report.

Up to this point, this writer has examined the testimony of witnesses to the love affair. But what did Lincoln himself say about his love for Ann? Mrs. Lincoln contends that he never once during their twenty-two years of marriage mentioned her name.[33] Miss Randall states, "There is no verified utterance by Lincoln, either oral or in writing that mentions Ann's name."[34] However, this writer found a quote in Isaac Arnold's biography in which Lincoln says, "I loved her dearly. She was a handsome girl and would have made a good loving wife. She was natural and quite intellectual, though not highly educated."[35] This utterance was witnessed by an Isaac Cogswell recognized in a footnote provided by the author. However, this writer found that Mr. Arnold has omitted a bibliography and no information other than this man's name is given. This writer could find no additional information as to the identification of Cogswell or any verification of this quote.

There is an absence of any written acknowledgement of Ann by Lincoln. This writer has examined a supposedly complete collection of Lincoln's letters and has found

[31]Tarbell, op. cit., p. 218.
[32]R. Randall, op. cit., p. 398-399.
[33]Stefan Lorant, The Life of Abraham Lincoln: A Short Illustrated Biography, p. 35.
[34]R. Randall, op. cit., p. 398.
[35]Isaac Arnold, Life of Lincoln, p. 43.

that only one letter exists during the period from April 28, 1832[36] to June 13, 1836.[37] There exists only a report on a road survey dated June, 1834, to which Lincoln signed his name. Carl Sandburg relates that there are three letters dated during the year 1835; but they shed no light on his love.[38] There was in existence a stone from the New Salem neighborhood dug up in 1890 near the Lincoln and Berry store by the grandson of Bowling Green (a friend of Lincoln), according to affidavits. On the stone has been chiseled the legend: A Lincoln Ann Rutledge were betrothed here July 4, 1833.[39] It is interesting to note that if the stone is authentic and the previously quoted Mr. Rankin's testimony is accurate, Ann waited two years before confiding in his mother about her engagement to Lincoln.

From all the information amassed by Herndon two things remained clearest in the minds of the witnesses: that Ann had been engaged to John McNamar, who was living in New Salem under the name of McNeil, and was not present when she died, and that Lincoln grieved over her death. Thomas agrees with the first statement concerning McNamar.[40] J.[41] and R.[42] Randall concur with both statements. While most testimonies agree Lincoln was saddened at the time of Ann's death, this writer has found many explanations as to the cause for this despondency. Robert Rutledge thought that Herndon, over the course of thirty years, had confused Lincoln's despondency over his broken engagement with Mary Todd with his grief over Ann's death.[43] Of the other explanations of his gloom, one contends he was overburdened by increased law study; another states he was physically ill; still another brings up the thought that he always took deaths hard. Although there is disagreement by historians and witnesses on why he grieved, all the historians this writer has examined reject the theory this grief bordered on insanity. Of the witnesses who support the insanity theory, one was Minton Graham, whose unreliability has already been examined. Another was Robert Rutledge who, as before, changed his testimony. He once wrote Herndon he could not testify to Lincoln's mental suffering from personal knowledge. Another time he declared,"…the effect upon Mr. Lincoln's mind was terrible…."[44] A Mrs. Bennet Abell, with whom Lincoln stayed at the time of Ann's death, said, "…he was not crazy but he was very desponding."[45]

Another and perhaps the most controversial aspect of the romance is Herndon's contention that Lincoln always loved Ann and no one else. Barton contends that it was McNamar who supplied Herndon with this information, the very same McNamar who denied any knowledge of the romance.[46] In any case, one year later, the Lincoln who supposedly never loved any other woman was courting a Miss Mary Owens. Lincoln

[36]John Nicolay and J. Hay, Abraham Lincoln: Complete Works. Comprising His Speeches, Letters, State Papers and Miscellaneous Writings, Vol. I p. 1.
[37]Ibid., p.7.
[38] Carl Sandburg, Abraham. Lincoln: The Prairie Years and The War Years, p. 44.
[39]Carl Sandburg, Lincoln Collector: The Story of Oliver Barrett's Great Private Collection, p. 133.
[40]Thomas, op. cit., p. 50.
[41]J. Randall, op. cit., p. 54-55.
[42]R. Randall, op. cit., p. 397.
[43]Ibid.,p. 398.
[44]J. Randall, op. cit., p. 54.
[45]R. Randall, op. cit., p. 403, as taken from clipping from The Menard Axis, February 15, 1862; Mrs. Bennet Abell to Herndon, February 15, 1867, Herndon-Weik mss.
[46]Barton, op. cit., p. 220.

writes in a letter dated May 7, 1837, "I know I should be much happier with you than I am...."[47] He did form a favorable impression of Mary in 1833 when Ann was still alive.[48] Furthermore, when Lincoln was trying to decide whether or not to marry Mary Todd, he confided in Joshua Speed. If his uncertainty was due to his love of Ann, his letters to Speed do not reveal it. When Herndon delivered his lecture Speed declared it "...was all new to him."[49]

In spite of all the studies of the romance which followed Herndon's original efforts, no contemporary evidence of the romance has been uncovered.

---

[47]Nicolay and Hay, op. cit., p. 16.
[48]R. Randall, op. cit., p. 399.
[49]Barton, op. cit., p. 224.

# CONCLUSION

When doing research on the romance, I found innumerable sources on Lincoln's life which dealt with the Lincoln-Rutledge romance. The problem I encountered was that most authors used Herndon's writings as their main source of information, particularly those authors who published prior to 1930. They did not have the benefit of the extensive study of Herndon's papers done in the 1940s. Whether it is a result of this or not, I concluded that these authors were generally less critical of the romance than authors who did have access to the study. It is, therefore, my hope that by extensive criticism of Herndon and his sources of information, I have, in turn, questioned the accuracy of those authors who based their information upon his sources.

From my research, I have found that the Lincoln-Rutledge romance cannot be judged as simply fact or fiction. Each aspect of the romance has to be considered separately and judged on the reliability of the information pertaining to it.

Concerning Lincoln's love of Ann and his engagement to her, I concluded that this aspect of the romance comes under the classification of uncertainty. There is circumstantial evidence supporting the theory of his engagement, i.e., the stone, which could classify it as possibility. However, the numerous testimonies of ear and eyewitnesses who disagree must lower the theory of his love and engagement to uncertainty. That Lincoln loved Ann cannot be rejected entirely. There are those who support the theory. It can only be doubted due to the testimonies which disagree. Hence my conclusion of uncertainty.

That Lincoln grieved at the time of Ann's death, I consider a fact. From what I discovered, there is general agreement that he was despondent; the controversy centers on exactly why and to what degree. His grief, then, cannot be used to support the theory he loved Ann; why he grieved is uncertain. There are those witnesses such as Mentor Graham, who would have the world believe it, while others, such as Mrs. Abell, for example, deny any such report. Again, here is a case of two eyewitnesses who disagree.

The assertion that the memory of Ann Rutledge had an everlasting effect upon Lincoln I conclude as uncertainty also, for there are two witnesses who disagree: Mrs. Lincoln and McNamar. I am more inclined, however, to reject the theory entirely, and attribute it to Herndon's tendency to exaggerate which I have concluded from his writings. The use of this theory to explain Lincoln's melancholia in later life seems too unfounded, since no words or actions of Lincoln ever suggested this. This is my personal belief. However, historically, it must be classified as uncertainty.

There is one thing this term paper has taught me with regard to Lincoln himself. For such a respected man who holds such a revered place in our history, so little is known about his personality. I believe that Lincoln-Rutledge romance is not valuable as a clue to Lincoln's character; a little more knowledge of his character would help prove the accuracy or inaccuracy of this romance. Only this knowledge could prove whether Lincoln was capable of living twenty- two years with a woman he never loved. Only this knowledge could prove if the death of a loved one could drive him nearly insane.    I feel that due to an absence of this knowledge this romance has to be considered uncertainty, and until such information is discovered, if it ever will be, the romance will remain an uncertainty.

# PRIMARY SOURCES

Hertz, Emanuel, ed., <u>The Hidden Lincoln: From the Letters and Papers of</u> <u>William H. Herndon</u>. New York: The Viking Press, 1938, 461 pp.

Nicolay, John G. and John Hay, ed., <u>Abraham Lincoln: Complete Works,</u> <u>Comprising His Speeches, Letters, State Papers and Miscellaneous</u> <u>Writings</u>. Vol. I, New York: The Century Company, 1894, 695 pp.

Sandburg, Carl, <u>Lincoln Collector: The Story of Oliver G. Barrett's</u> <u>Great Private Collection</u>. New York: Harcourt, Brace and Company, 1950, 344 pp.

## SECONDARY SOURCES

Arnold, Isaac, <u>The Life of Abraham Lincoln</u>. Chicago: Jansen, McClung and Company, 1884, 462 pp.

Barton, William E., <u>The Life of Abraham Lincoln</u>. Vol. I, Indianapolis: The Bobbs  Merrill  Company, 1925, 517 pp.

Donald, David H., <u>Lincoln's Herndon</u>. New York, Alfred A. Knopf, Inc., 1948, 392 pp.

Lorant, Stefan, <u>The Life of Abraham Lincoln: A Short Illustrated Biography</u>. New York:  The McGraw-Hill Book Company Inc., 1954, 160 pp.

Malone, Dumas, ed., <u>Dictionary of American Biography</u>. Vol. VIII, New York: Charles Scribner's Sons, 1932, 612 pp.

Randall, James G., <u>Mr. Lincoln</u>. New York: Dodd, Mead and Company, 1957, 392 pp.

Randall, Ruth P., <u>Mary Lincoln: Biography of a Marriage</u>. Boston: Little, Brown and Company, 1953, 555 pp.

Sandburg, Carl, <u>Abraham Lincoln: The Prairie Years and the War Years</u>. New York:  Harcourt, Brace and Company, 1954, 762 pp.

Tarbell, Ida M., <u>In the Footsteps of the Lincolns</u>. New York: Harper and Sons, 1924, 418 pp.

Thomas, Benjamin P., <u>Abraham Lincoln, A Biography</u>. New York: Alfred A. Knopf, Inc., 1952, 548 pp.

# CHAPTER X

# HISTORIOGRAPHY

The outcome of research, interviewing, hours of reading, note taking, analysis of sources, and fitting together of ideas is the development of conclusions. These conclusions should touch the writer's deepest thoughts. Do these conclusions strengthen beliefs? Do they support your generation's opinions? Altogether, how do they describe your generation? This last question brings us to the third and final process of history, "historiography."

The writing or telling of past events, episodes, or situations, historiography utilizes the processes of both historical research and historical method. The historian recreates the past by way of reconstruction and synthesis. These two operations are the "building blocks" of historiography. Suffice to say that historiography is "…the imaginative reconstruction of the past from data derived by that process…and…the synthesizing of such data into historical exposition and narratives" (Gottschalk, 1969, pp. 48-49).

It is important to understand that an event or series of events once completed may not be repeated. Therefore, the word, "reconstruction," applies to the rebuilding of the event or events by the historian who has studied them. In reality, the historian has actually "recreated" the happenings. Let us see reconstruction in action. A thousand years from now, scholars will still be examining our world of today. They will be analyzing primary and secondary sources available to them. They will be evaluating information and coming to conclusions about you, me, and our world. How do you think they will reconstruct our actions and behavior? Will they reconstruct our standards to match their standards of behavior and conduct? Will they be able to see us as we see ourselves? Their reconstructions will depend on what they believe our world was like.

The historian's "synthesis" is the finished product. It reflects a viewpoint or an interpretation of your society. The scholar must present a point of view. He or she owes this to the readers. The writer may not simply record all the primary and secondary evidence or come to conclusions without taking a stand for or against you. Anyone who merely summarizes the work of previous writers is not advancing the study of history. All of us should take some stand on an issue after we have examined the available evidence and formulated our conclusions. Of course, one hopes that the synthesis of some portion of history will be as objective as possible. Even if the writer dislikes young people, let us hope that he or she does not let that prejudice interfere with a fair and impartial treatment of your generation. Otherwise, the writer is guilty of letting his or her emotions rule. The writer may lose objectivity. The historian's personal convictions or philosophy of life may be opposite to your generation's. If he or she colors conclusions to fit personal outlook, the historian has deceived readers. He or she has ceased to be professional. The writer may ignore some materials regardless of their historical credibility and reliability because they could alter conclusions. If so, the historian is guilty of misusing the material, the topic, and of formulating a prejudicial viewpoint. Since he or she knows certain sources will change conclusions, the writer may exclude opposing beliefs. The reader may never know that the writer has overlooked the references to the good deeds that your age group is doing for its country. Instead, the historian may mislead the public and may describe the negative behavior of your generation.

Going one step further, the problem of preconceived conclusions highlights the need the historian may have to justify beliefs. Instead of coming to a conclusion based upon the survey of evidence, the historian may insist upon proving something to be certain. He or she may have found insufficient evidence, but will continue searching for any evidence that will strengthen prejudices. Unfortunately, the reader may never suspect the professional of deceit. The reader may believe that he or she is helpless against the academic power of the trained historian.

What is the answer to the problem of syntheses based upon prejudiced conclusions or interpretations based upon preestablished convictions? The solution is simple, provided emotions do not interfere with intellectual pursuit. Let all reliable sources of information lead the historical investigator to the answers to questions. Let the evidence lead that individual to additional sources. Let the individual not ignore any evidence that runs counter to personal beliefs. Of course, this is easier said than done. Older people are not likely to blame themselves for any faults young people may have.

If you are doing wonderful things for your society and nation, some may try to take full credit by citing all the evidence that points to how much they have helped you to be the great generation you are. If yours is a generation filled with delinquency and social misbehavior, they are not as likely to reveal the primary and secondary sources that place blame on the older generation. It is you who are at fault. Some go about proving this in history texts. They cite all the evidence of your misconduct and totally ignore adult misbehavior. This synthesis, this interpretation, in other words, this finished product is technically correct. It contains a complete bibliography of sources, sufficient footnoting of primary and secondary material, external and internal criticisms and appropriate conclusions. What we have is still historical deceit. You have become the victim, the target of that synthesis.

Synthesis, also, is directly related to the particular selection of sources the historian uses to best point out evidence. Preparing a historical paper, you may have notes written on many index cards. You must select from the cards those bits of information that will most effectively and persuasively support your synthesis of the happening and your point of view. The selection of primary and secondary evidence continues to be vital. Every time you use sources for your topic, you have selected those works. However, in reality, perhaps, these particular works are the only sources available to you at the present time. So, there may be very little selectivity on your part. It is for this reason that many professional writers of history revise their syntheses at different stages in their lives. As new evidence is unearthed and more materials are made available to the public, a greater range of selectivity is possible.

Furthermore, syntheses and interpretations will vary depending upon historians of the future. Perhaps, some will present us as cruel, barbarous people. Maybe, others will find primarily good in our civilization. To what extent their emotions will govern their selection of evidence and formulation of conclusions is impossible for us to know. What historians of the future write about our world will also depend not only upon their personality makeups, but upon the type of society and the kind of world in which they will be living. How much will their societal values influence their writing, their conclusions, reconstructions, and syntheses?

Suppose the world of the future will not allow any form of human slavery. Will historians look back at our world as a world of human misery and persecution? Suppose the world of tomorrow will consist of a massive system of slavery? Will historians see us as weaklings, unable to measure up to their concept of greatness and strength?

We think of ourselves as a democratic nation. We often read in history about the glorious world of the ancient Greeks, particularly the Athenians. We cite these people as an example of an enlightened society. Were not the Athenians slave holders? Are we not employing in our interpretation or synthesis of Athenian history modern concepts of democracy? Were these people democratic according to our standards or to theirs?

As a historian matures in life, his or her attitude toward society and its values may change. It may be that as a young writer, one saw the evils of the world more vividly than one does now. The scholar may have become more or less courageous about life. What was once so serious is now laughed at. These changes of attitude may come to an entire civilization. For example, a thousand years from now historians' judgments of our society will depend on whether tomorrow's society will honor its elders or its young. If society becomes youth centered, perhaps, it will judge you very differently than if it reverts to the American colonial code of honor and respect for the older generation.

As we examine our history, we find constructions, syntheses, and interpretations followed by newer reconstructions, systhesis and reinterpretations. For example, were we fair to Native Americans during earlier periods of our development? How did colonial writers portray Native Americans? What do modern scholars write about their treatment? In the twenty-first century, the United States seems to be growing more humanitarian. The injustices toward Native Americans have been shown in movies and on television programs. However, in a thousand years, will Native Americans, as a people with their own history, have survived?

The topic of reinterpretation leads to the examination of alternative points of view. What view do you take in the study of history? You may take a "revisionist" view. That is, you find a new path such as a fresh look at or "review" of the contributions of Native Americans to the cultural life of our nation. Perhaps, having examined the chapter on academic disciplines, you may decide to choose an economic interpretation of history. You may decide to study the history of wants and needs of society and how demand for a certain good or service was satisfied during a period in American or World history. You may follow a political approach in which you are interested in the roots of power and influence of governing bodies. By taking a cultural approach to the study of history you focus on the development of values, beliefs, attitudes, and behavior within a particular culture. From a sociological perspective, you may prefer "inclusive" history which means the study of such groups as women, Afro- Americans, Latinos, and others. What about a philosophical or religious approach to the study of history? Are you interested in how the peoples of the earth have interpreted their purposes in life and their spiritual journeys?

Whatever approach you choose, careful selection of sources is an important aspect of historiography. It is the part of one's work for which one should feel most proud and sure of oneself. Let us remember, however, that we may stand by our constructions, syntheses, interpretations, and points of view with firmness, but not with finality. We must be able to alter our points of view as new evidence is discovered and analyzed.

Historiography is, also, the process by which one examines and reviews constructions, syntheses, points of view, and interpretations of past and present historians. Historiography covers the writing of history from ancient civilization to modern or present time. In this aspect, the historiographer is concerned with the question: Why does a writer of history choose a particular interpretation of an event, series of events, or portion of history? By analyzing syntheses written about and/or during selected periods of time, the historiographer notes the reflective nature of historiography. It reflects the attributes of learned behavior in culture that influence construction, synthesis, and interpretation of the past.

For the above reasons, there may not be absolute reality resulting from the study and writing of history, only interpretation of what we believe is reality. A historian should strive to be objective. However, that historian is still a human being with human weaknesses, biases, and prejudices. Subjective feelings about his or her generation, society, or concepts of right and wrong may find their way into a final reconstruction and synthesis. Therefore, the most we should expect from a historian is "integrity" defined as honesty and truthfulness to oneself. If you refer back to Chapter III, "In Search of Truth," you will find the following advice by Polonius to his son: "This above all, to thine own self be true...." Integrity and objectivity are what we want from any historian regardless of race, religion, or national origin, regardless of whether or not his or her interpretations of history agree with ours.

# FOR FURTHER STUDY

Examine your own values. What would you write in a paper called "This I Believe"? For what reasons would you be willing to leave home, stand against injustice, lose a friend?

On page 198 of the work entitled, <u>The Fall of the Dynasties: The Collapse of the Old Order 1905-1922</u>, by Edmond Taylor, published by Doubleday and Company in 1963, appears the following:

> Some of the original controversies about the origins of the crime at Sarajevo have died down as more information became available to historians but there is still enough obscurity about certain important details to sustain quite divergent interpretation. The viewpoint that the assassination was essentially a local plot that spontaneously generated in the minds of young Princip and his fellow conspirators, to which some irresponsible nationalist elements in Belgrade gave rather offhand assistance, cannot be formally disproved. Neither can the contrary hypothesis that the murder of the heir to the Hapsburg throne was systematically planned at a high government level in Belgrade, or even in St. Petersburg. The most convincing version, at least to a journalist who has had occasion to investigate---or to cover the investigation---of later political assassinations in Europe, lies between the two extremes, and is based in the main on the conclusions reached by the Italian historian, Luigi Albetini, after exhaustive documentary research and interviews of surviving key witnesses.
>
> By permission of the publisher.

Who was actually responsible for the assassinations of Archduke Ferdinand and his wife?  Examine the origins of World War I given in a world history text.  Compare the reasons given for the assassinations with the version offered by Mr. Taylor.

A reprint of an engraving by Paul Revere appears on the following page. His synthesis suggests an organized British attack on unarmed civilians.  The event is known as "The Boston Massacre."

Paul Revere, Jr., American, 1734-1818. Christian Remick, American, 1726-after 1783. *The Boston Massacre, 1770* Engraving, hand colored with watercolor and gold pigment by Christian Remick.  Sight (image and text): 26.0 x 33.0 cm (10 ¼ x 13 in.) Frame: 36.2 x 33.0 (14 ¼ x 13 in.) Museum of Fine Arts Boston. Gift of Watson Grant Cutter, 67.1165.  Photograph c [2009] Museum of Fine Arts Boston.

Photo courtesy of the Library of Congress.

Notice that Chappel's interpretation of the "Massacre" gives the impression that the civilians prepared for battle.

# CHAPTER XI

## THE IMPORTANCE OF THE COMPUTER

Inspiration for the writing of this chapter has come from Professor Richard Kearney, Electronic Resource Librarian, William Paterson University, Wayne, New Jersey. Listening to Professor Kearney, I realize the world of electronic research is so complex that it requires the expertise of a librarian. Thus, the focus of this chapter is on the treatment of sources of information, obtained directly or indirectly from the computer, according to the processes of history.

Years ago, as a college student, I remember doing research at the Fifth Avenue and 42$^{nd}$ Street branch of the New York City Public Library system. This particular branch is, perhaps, one of the largest libraries in any city within the United States. What I remember vividly was the enormity of trays within the card catalog room. They contained the bibliographic entries and call numbers of the library's entire collection of primary and secondary sources. Bibliographic citations were typed on 3" by 5" cards. There were many trays for each letter of the alphabet. Each tray measured 20" in length and housed up to one hundred cards. One could search for a source in one of three ways: by author, title, or subject matter.

How well I recall having to wait for someone to finish using the tray I needed. Few people bothered to return trays to the correct wall bins. Imagine the time it took just to find the correct card! Having found it, I had to fill out a form identifying myself and the card's bibliographic entry as well as its call numbers and letters. There was no screen available to examine related material. Had I wanted to research further, I would have had to repeat the process of obtaining the tray which contained the appropriate citation, call numbers, and letters. Even subject matter trays were scattered and unavailable to me. Imagine walking around this great room and peeking at trays other people were using in order to find the right one! It took hours to accumulate enough "call slips" to make the trip to the library worthwhile.

Holding those precious call slips, I had to wait in line in the adjoining room to present them to the receiving clerk. Having spent hours in the card catalog room, I had to decide whether to wait my turn or leave and return another day or evening. When I did hand in the call slips, the clerk gave a separate paper with a number on it to me. I had to find a seat in this enormous room and wait for my number to appear on a large screen on the front wall. When my number appeared, what could I expect? All sources I had requested were available. Some were being used. None of them were available. I had to return as many times as it took to secure the material I needed. Even though all the items in the reference room had to remain in that great hall, anyone using the material I needed could have left trays on any of the tables. I could not have known that until they were returned to the clerk's desk.

Recently, I revisited the same room in the Fifth Avenue Library. The trays filled to capacity with bibliographic data disappeared. Instead, they have been replaced by computers for anyone to use to do research. Call slips are located next to each computer. One must still fill out the correct information and hand the forms to the clerk. One must still wait in the adjoining room for the number to appear on the front screen.

Now, compare my experience with yours. Using your computer, move the "mouse," depress several keys, and as if by magic---you have before your eyes a wealth of entries within seconds! It is amazing how all these sources of information are displayed on the screen so quickly. And, by using your printer, you have the luxury of being able to change electronic data into printed format.

As you use your computer to do electronic search or research, you have choices: Examine electronic library catalogs and indices belonging to school, public, governmental, or private libraries. Conduct your research on the Web. Do both. The "Web," also referred to as the World Wide Web, (WWW) "… is simply information that is connected or linked in a sort of web." (Ackerman and Hartman, 1991, p.1). All information is carried by thousands upon thousands of networks which are connected to a master Internet. Thus, you access information from the Web via the Internet (Ackerman, p.1). Use any number of search engines which index publicly accessible web sites. A "search engine" is "…a collection of programs that gathers information from the Web, indexes it, and puts it in a database" (Ackerman, p.434). There is an enormous difference between a library catalog or index and a "search engine" in content, indexing, and mission. Libraries set publicly known standards for cataloging and indexing sources of information by category such as: type of book, journal, magazine, newspaper, pamphlet, etc. Through indexing, one may research articles needed for studying or writing. On the other hand, search engines have rules for cataloging and indexing that are, at best, vague because it is very expensive to properly catalog sources according to library standards. Despite attempts to appeal to the serious investigator and scholar, a search engine company, no matter what experience you have using it, is not solely in business to help you. It is, also, in business to make a financial profit. The library has no financially hidden agenda. Its collection is selected for you as consumer, student, or writer of history. In sum, the Web is not a library.

It is important to understand that publishing on the Web is very easy. There is neither quality control nor a "gate keeper." Any individual or group, from the most prestigious, scholarly publisher to an elementary school child with access to web publishing tools, may produce a web site. Web hosting companies make material available to the public. Search engines will then index the site through their use of "spidering" programs that continuously scour the public web for new and updated sites and pages. The specific ranking of sites in the results of a web search is private information. The search engine company does not have to inform the public as to the reason for the rank of a specific page in search results. A search engine company, therefore, regards its retrieval algorithms (set of rules) as proprietary (private property).

From your point of view as a serious researcher, a consumer of electronic search engines needs to retrieve the sources of information. A needed electronic entry may appear at or near the beginning, middle, or end of an enormous list of sources. That is why it is essential for you, as a researcher to use more then one search engine.  Also, each search engine has special databases and it is essential to learn to use these multiple databases.  Instead of relying on just one database, you have additional options which are important as you compare sources of information.  In one database, you may find what you want at the top of the list.  In another database, you may find the source somewhere further down the listing.  I must stress that you should ask for guidance from your electronic resource librarian.

It is important to read the search engine instructions so that you will be able to find the appropriate sources as you need them.  Remember that search engines are programmed to look for new entries and to add them continuously to their databases.  Unlike search engines "…directories are created and maintained by people, whereas search engines rely on spiders or robots to scour the Internet for links" (Ackerman, p. 98).  "Directories" are topical lists of Internet sources.  You should use more than one directory as you would use multiple search engine databases (Ackerman, p. 98).

Regardless of advances in electronic data technology taking place daily around the globe, information must be identified, examined, and analyzed according to the rules and guidelines of the processes of history.  Imagine a fully electronic library.  What is the same as the traditional library?  It is the cataloging and indexing of library sources, now online.  Imagine the World Wide Web with millions upon millions of entries cited in search engines.  What is significant is the enormity of source material.  In today's world of electronic data, there are endless electronic shelves of pamphlets, documents, prints, photographs, as well as other types of sources of information created by unknown or unrecognized individuals, groups, or organizations.  Perhaps, one of these sources may contain information that is vital to your study or writing.  Perhaps, it may be worthless because it may contain falsified, distorted, or non-credible, plagiarized information.  No matter what material is displayed on your screen, there must be a way to find and identify the origin of the source by name.  Whether by footnote or by some other means of documenting its existence, you must establish authentic identity.  Even if the identity is hidden on purpose, do not give up.  The computer may help you to uncover the identity in ways unheard of before the age of computers.

Keep in mind that stored within the World Wide Web and connected through the global Internet, are two main sets of data.  One: bibliographic entries.  Two: narrative, artistic, and oral material.  As you explore these sets of data, refer to operations within each process of history: historical research, historical method, and historiography.  The operations are the same for electronic as well as non-electronic data.  For historical research, data obtained from the computer must be classified as primary, secondary, or left uncertain as to the nature of the source.  It is essential to identify the origin of the data.  Is it an individual, group, organization, business or governmental agency?  Does the source have a governing or editorial board?  Is there a way of contacting the individual or group in charge electronically by e-mail, telephone, or letter?

Using the historical method, critically examine and evaluate each electronic source both externally and internally.  You should try to uncover the history, background, and character of the individual or group in question. What are their aims, goals, purposes of formation, and beliefs? If there are electronic films, photographs, or other kinds of visual and oral material, examine each critically as well. Using digital cameras and cell phones, one is able to film and photograph people and events and display them across the World Wide Web. It is conceivable that these materials may not have been approved by traditional media, by government, nor by organizational authorities. Perhaps, at this moment, people across the globe are filming or photographing scenes of injustice, cruelty, or illegality in any institution at any level and source of power within society: economic, political, and social. Will that evidence be displayed on the computer screen by those who have access to publishing technology? Is the evidence credible (believable) and reliable (trustworthy)? You may learn the answers as you compare electronic and non-electronic data. What conclusions do you reach from the sources you have analyzed?

Historiography, the final process of history, requires that you synthesize your evidence in order to write or discuss your findings and point of view. Whatever the combination and ratio of traditional to electronic sources, you must select the best evidence that supports your hypothesis or main purpose of your study or writing. Selectivity of electronic sources should be treated in the same way and held to the same standards of external and internal criticisms and appropriate conclusions as non electronic sources. In developing and preparing your study, use standard 4" by 6" index cards for bibliographic entries, note taking, and reactions, all of which you need to finalize your work. There is, in addition, a new electronic tool to print and file bibliographic citations, notes, and reactions. It is a process designed to record, separate, and store information for the three sets of cards. The process is referred to as "bibliographic management software." This tool enables you to use any library of your choice and to transfer information directly on to your personal computer. If you are able to obtain this tool, why not try both methods, traditional and electronic, to see which one is appropriate for you? For a fuller explanation of the use of index cards in studying or writing history, read Chapter XIX, "*Preparing A Historical Paper.*"

There are limitations to the availability of electronic data. If you find a bibliographic entry of interest, you may be unable to obtain the complete narrative from which the entry was taken. It may be from a journal, magazine, newspaper article, or from other material, which for some reason, has not been scanned. Unless you are able to find the complete narrative from a library catalog which has scanned the material, you may have to write or visit the library which has a complete copy. Scanning data is expensive and time consuming. Those responsible for placing the material on the World Wide Web may have chosen not to incur the expense. There are thousands upon thousands of articles that were published years ago. Perhaps, no one in management of the publishing companies had the interest, time, nor money to spend in order to transfer the material to online format. Furthermore, some of those publishing companies may no longer be in business.

Perhaps, the data you seek is in the online catalog of a library to which you do not have access. If you are not enrolled in a particular college or university that houses the data, you will be denied access. However, you may be able to gain access by a letter of introduction and/or payment of a special fee. Perhaps, the library may be in a foreign country that will not give you permission to examine the data. What about rare documents, letters, notes, etc.? These archival materials may be too precious to scan. They may have been placed in special archival rooms or in storage. Even historical works on college library shelves (stacks) may not have been scanned. You may have to physically travel to the facility that houses the data. At the present time, there are hundreds of thousands of sources being published. They will not all be scanned for viewing on computer screens. There are many small publishers across the globe that lack the resources to scan their material electronically. This is not to say that their material is less important. On the contrary, smaller publishers, like any other independent producers of information, may offer evidence that is not available in main stream media. Of course, external and internal criticism will reveal the historical worth of the evidence.

A serious and disturbing limitation being placed on electronic data is censorship of electronic information. If governmental and private agencies across the globe continue to control publishing of material on the World Wide Web, then traditional methods of obtaining information by interview, letter, telephone call, etc. should be undertaken. If censorship continues, computer sources may lose credibility and reliability. They may become standardized, controlled, and less likely to contain fresh, original, spontaneous, or unabridged data.

In closing, as I look back to the days and evenings I spent researching and note taking in the Fifth Avenue Public Library, I realize how essential computer and electronic technology have become in the quest for historical truth. As a tool for studying and writing history, the computer is invaluable. It brings to our screens an endless variety of bibliographic and historical data from every corner of our planet through the magic of the World Wide Web and Internet. Perhaps, one day, computer programming will enable us, using our lap tops wherever we happen to be, to create complete sets of bibliographic entries, notes, and reactions. Perhaps, the computer will automatically examine those notes both externally and internally, draw conclusions, reconstruct, and synthesize our findings, as well as electronically develop our points of view. Think of it. Our entire study will be done electronically! Who knows? Only time and the calculus of technological change will tell.

# CHAPTER XII

# GENEALOGY

What do you know about your family roots? Portions of your family's history lie buried in the graves of your ancestors. Have you ever inquired about your father's or mother's life? What were they like as children? What were your grandparents and their parents like when they were growing up? Your family's history has its own rich and interesting story to tell.

In this world of unforeseen change, there is opportunity for you to discover your place in the stream of history. You may do this by learning about your family ancestry. Genealogy, the study of family history, is a branch of knowledge from which you may derive much satisfaction. As long as you accept yourself, you may accept your ancestors who lived on earth before you. It is both desirable and healthy to establish some connection and identity with the past. You live in an age in which the extended family has separated into smaller units. Often, the unit itself separates and members move away in varied directions. In earlier times, this was not so. It may give you a feeling of permanence to know about and understand your ancestors and their culture.

You may believe that your ancestors did nothing worthy of recording in historical records. How do you know? Are you certain? What historical investigation of your genealogy have you undertaken to establish such a conclusion? It is not important for your ancestors to have done anything as individual leaders. Their participation in the life of their communities is a significant contribution to civilization. It should be reason enough for you to be proud of your genealogy. We all contribute to civilization while we live. After death, we leave something of ourselves to history. Will it be necessary for us to have performed miracles in order to be judged favorably by our posterity?

Your mother's and father's ancestors left their individual marks on earth. They worked with others to build the roads, bridges, and buildings which we use. They tilled the land that feeds and sustains us. They developed the industries upon which we depend so heavily for our goods and services. They built the foundation of our civilization. They transmitted their culture and handed down their music, art, dance, drama, literature: in short, their way of life to us.

Thomas Wolfe wrote the book, <u>You Can't Go Home Again</u>. However, you may "go home again" to seek a part of you that will never die, your heritage. It is difficult to define the word, "heritage." Used in the context of genealogical investigation, it means the sum of all your ancestors' experiences which have shaped and molded your family's history. All their sweat, joy, sorrow, and tears blend into a final inheritance which only you, by right of birth, possess. You own that inheritance; no one may take it from you.

Who among you has not some ancestor who suffered a deprived life in order that yours could be more secure, peaceful, or happy? Who among you has an ancestor on either side of your family whose life seemed unfulfilled while he or she was alive? Nevertheless, that same individual's efforts were recorded somewhere in history as part of the great, human story of the historical contribution of labor. Voluntary and involuntary laborers came to the shores of Colonial America and later, to the United States. They worked for the benefit of those who exploited them. Notice, however, the results. Many ended their bondage within a few years, and after their terms of servitude were over started new lives. Others had to wait a longer time. Still others, whose bondage was "durante, vita," for life or perpetual, had to wait for what seemed an endless period for freedom. Let us affirm that with the ending of slavery, such an episode in the history of humanity will never again be repeated.

Now is the time for us to look back to our ancestors with a feeling of gratitude because we have been spared the pain and suffering which they had endured. However, some people will not accept the truth of their heritage. They may even attempt to change or conceal their genealogy. They may feel that humanity will scorn them unless they disguise their heritage. What a pity! What a denial of truth! And think of all the time and energy spent on falsifying, distorting, or denying records. What may lie beneath these actions? Hidden feelings of guilt, inadequacy, or unworthiness? Yet, others, for example, may experience the joy of learning that their ancestors retained national, religious, racial, or ethnic identity and began a new way of life for themselves and their posterity. Perhaps, they found the answer to their dreams in an entirely new land and in a strange culture.

What connection does the study of genealogy have to the study of history? We are likely to build interest in the past of different individuals, groups, or societies if we show interest in our own backgrounds, our own ancestries. We, who share genealogical interest, become committed to the goal of knowing our own heritage and, therefore, our own histories. We are not afraid of uncovering mysteries from the past. On the contrary, we welcome the challenge. For us, genealogical research may become a personal involvement, a step closer to our self-understanding.

Perhaps, the best way to begin your genealogy is with what you know. This information may be recorded graphically in several interesting ways. There are models which may be used, none requiring too much artistic skill, but all depending a good deal on your imagination and industry. A popular graphic form among genealogists is the fan-shaped, family tree. The advantage of using this form is that you may see the entire family at a glance. You will need a large piece of paper for this particular shape. Reserve one-half of the fan for your father's family and the other half for your mother's family. Whether you are male or female, begin with information about yourself. Place your full name at the base of the open fan. Since this construction is your personal genealogy, do not include the names of any of your brothers or sisters. As you draw lines on your chart, extend them back as far as you are able to go in tracing your family genealogy. Below the line, record at least the following information for each of your ancestors: date of birth, marriage, and death.

Once you have listed all those members in your family of whom you are personally aware, you are ready to research further for background information. How do you start your genealogical investigation? Begin your genealogical study by interviewing family members and by keeping a log in which you record the name of each person interviewed, date, and place of interview. Tape the interview as a record of oral history. Question interviewees on their life experiences from earliest recollections to the present. Interview relatives of all ages. In this way, you will understand how the family is connected by values, beliefs, attitudes, and behavior. The topics may range from childhood memories, teen years, adult life, working careers, social life, problems, and any other topics you wish to explore. If a family member refuses to discuss a particular topic, respect the interviewee's right to remain silent. If any members of your family are unavailable for questioning in person, you may write or contact them by telephone or e-mail. As you develop your log for each interviewee, try to ask the same question of each person who witnessed a happening or an event so that you may compare responses. You have the responsibility to test the information for external accuracy and internal bias or prejudice. Collect photographs and relics of interest to you and your family members.

Having completed research and investigation on members of your family, turn your attention to the surroundings and environment in which you and your family members have lived and/or are living. Become familiar with available primary and secondary sources of information in the localities in which you and your family members reside. Just by taking walks, you become acquainted with historic landmarks such as old houses, public buildings, and business establishments. Why not look at an old street map of your neighborhood? The importance of local history should not be ignored. In one way or another, it may have shaped the course of your family's history.

Visit your local government offices which may house valuable information about your ancestors. If you are unable to meet with responsible keepers of records, write letters to them and ask all your questions. As you become interested in your heritage, you will undoubtedly meet local genealogists who are interested in helping you to learn more about your family's history.

Local religious and social organizations keep records of their memberships. They may publish journals, newspapers, or newsletters which may contain some interesting features about your ancestors. You may interview older members who remember your relatives. However, you you should not forget your responsibility to test for external authenticity and internal reliability. Try to determine whether a person you are interviewing actually knew your ancestors. If so, try to learn about any personal feelings or attitudes this member had about your ancestors. How did feelings affect the account of your ancestors' experiences?

As you increase your knowledge of local history, you will soon expand your interest to include the study of county history. In certain states, county records are more complete than are local records. Primary sources such as wills, deeds, and letters of administration regarding family estates may be housed in county archives. Of course, it is important to read what is available concerning the history of the county in which your ancestors lived. Perhaps, your community was once a large tract of land that was split into separate communities. Your town may have joined with another to form a larger political unit. If so, the records in your county historical library may reveal the necessary information you seek regarding your family's life experiences.

From county history you will want to go to state sources of information. If you plan to visit the state capital, write letters or email so that you will learn which agency in the state government houses the evidence you need. Histories of your state may give you additional insight into the political, economic, cultural, and social problems your family members may have faced during the administration of a particular governor and session of a state legislature. Laws passed during the period in which you are interested were bound to affect your ancestors.

Your research will eventually bring you to the focal point of national life, United States history. You should consider the reasons for passage of acts by the United States Congress. For example, national acts covering immigration at certain times during our country's development were not always beneficial to the needy foreigner waiting for permission to enter or remain in the United States. There have been periods in our nation's history when our government was afraid of opening admission to certain groups. You could try to find out why. By inquiring, you may understand and appreciate the behavior and actions of your ancestors in a new country. You may also learn why our government acted as it did.

Extensive records regarding immigrants are maintained by the United States Government. They are generally housed in special collections that our national government provides. You may have to write to the Department of Immigration in Washington, D.C. in order to decide which place you should visit. It is also likely that some records regarding your ancestors' arrival are available at the place of entry. For example, if your ancestors arrived in the Untied States at one of the seaports in California, it is very likely that the port city, county, or even the state of California houses vital information. In the case of immigrants who arrived before the establishment of the United States, records of these newcomers were most likely kept by the local and county governments or by governmental agencies in the thirteen colonies.

Your research may continue across the ocean to places of birth of your foreign ancestors. Naturally, in tracing your genealogy to a foreign country, you should become familiar with its historical development. For example, disputes with one or more countries might have resulted in wars. As a consequence of war, the citizenship of your ancestors might have changed. The victor might have required that all records be brought to the capital of the victorious nation. Other essential records might have been transcribed into the language of the conqueror. Moreover, the names of birthplaces of your ancestors might have changed if a different country occupied your family members' town or village at the time of their birth.

Just imagine how exciting it could be for you to actually travel to a distant country and visit relatives. Even if you could not do this, think how rewarding it could be for you to write a letter, correspond via e-mail, and receive an encouraging reply. Even without a command of any foreign language, you could still have someone else translate the letters you write and receive. There may be a person in the receiving village or city who knows how to read and write English and who would be willing to read your letters to any of your non-English speaking relatives. Most exciting of all is the chance that there could be relatives your age. They could be very interested in hearing from you and in beginning a new friendship with you and your family. Today, there are opportunities for inexpensive travel to all parts of the world. Together with your foreign relatives you could continue the search for primary and secondary sources of information. At the same time, you could be encouraging them to become interested in tracing their own genealogy.

There are times when the search for truth may lead to tragic personal or group experiences. It may lead to evidence of murder, suicide, rape, mass extermination, or slavery. What have become of the eyewitnesses, records, and documents? It may seem to you that no one is left to tell the story of the tragedy. So many wars have taken their toll on human life. So many disasters have spread human suffering and death far beyond the location of misfortune and dispute. Factual information may sometimes be beyond one's comprehension. But you should not give up the search. One survivor may be left who could shed light on the history and whereabouts of your family members.

When you consider the terrible loss of life and the destruction of property resulting from wars within the past one hundred years, it is a miracle that any primary or secondary sources are available. However, buried in the heap of destruction may be memoirs, diaries, or notebooks kept by those unfortunates of humanity. Because of human and climatic destruction, whole villages and cities lie in ruin. However, somewhere, some physical remains of the past may still exist. The artifacts that were never burned nor mutilated may lie unrecognized.

Whether you search in the United States or in a foreign country, you must test for the external accuracy of the information you find. Human errors in printing, typing, or writing may account for mistakes in the spelling of names or false identification of primary or secondary sources. The first and middle name and initial are extremely important in identifying the correct person. For purposes of external criticism, it is preferable to use the original language when you examine the correct spelling and complete names of ancestors and living family members. A student of your family's original language would be able to help you.

Internal evaluation and criticism, also, require that you study the materials carefully in order to detect false assumptions as well as prejudiced and biased accounts by eye witnesses and secondary writers. Do you detect any boasting, arrogance, or ridicule? By whom? Why? You may not be able to find the answers to these and similar questions, but, at least you have begun to expand your inquiry to include favorable and unfavorable accounts written by family members and outsiders.

Examination of official records such as wills, deeds, or letters of administration of property requires both external and internal evaluation. In the case of wills, try to examine the spelling of the names of all heirs. In wills written many years ago, perhaps items of sentimental or financial value were listed individually with instructions for giving them to specific heirs. Today, however, because of the unusually large variety of material possessions ranging from television sets to automobiles, these items are not generally listed separately. The entire estate (the total of all property, physical remains, and financial holdings) is normally left to the surviving spouse and/or is divided among the "next of kin."

The listing of each item may reveal inaccuracies in the dating of very old wills. You may discover that a particular item could not have been invented nor manufactured during the period under scrutiny. For example, a will dated 1820 which mentions a television set would come under suspicion. Wouldn't you say so? For this reason, any mementos, artifacts, and relics which your family possesses should be identified and labeled. If your relatives are able to supply answers for you, try to determine when and where the article under investigation was purchased. By whom and for whom was it bought?

What were the motives of those who left specific articles to designated heirs? By analyzing the sentimental and financial value of the items listed as well as the reasons why they were bequeathed to certain individuals, you automatically become involved in the process of internal criticism. Matters such as bias for and prejudice against particular heirs are bound to rise to the surface of your investigation.

What may result from genealogical research? For some people, the most exciting aspect may involve the making of new friends and family contacts. For others, the chance to travel to distant places may stir a desire for adventure. For still others, the connecting of family ties may draw them closer to their entire family and its genealogy. For those of you whose ancestors cannot be traced beyond your own generation or beyond the second or third generations, there is still pride in knowing that somewhere on this earth the lost generations of ancestors are not forgotten. Your attempt to establish some link, some identification with the past, may be an attempt to find them in spirit. As long as there are knowledge and memory, no one need live life in obscurity. You are the sum of all the contributions of all your ancestors. Just remembering their existence may make them an important part of your identity.

gr.-gr.-gr. grandfather

gr.-gr.-gr. grandmother

gr.-gr. grandfather

gr.-gr. grandmother

great grandfather

great grandmother

grandfather

grandmother

your father

your mother

yourself

born =
died =

married =
divorced =

# CHAPTER XIII

## CURRENT EVENTS

What do current events have to do with the processes of history? Once you understand these processes, the study of current affairs, current issues, or current history will have an entirely new meaning. Your hometown newspapers, your favorite commentator, your special current affairs magazine will no longer have exclusive control over your thoughts and over your reasoning power. Why not stop at this point to discuss with others how the method of historical inquiry may be applied to the history of local, national, and international news?

If you have thought about a new approach, share your ideas. What is happening now in another country or in the next town will in one way or another affect you, whether during peace time or war. Even the historian, who at this very moment may be analyzing primary sources of ancient Rome, should come out of seclusion to see what is happening to our society and to our world. How do you go about trying to understand the history of national and international events?

We may never succeed in understanding everything about current affairs, but we do isolate small areas of news. From where does the news come? You may read one or two newspapers. You may hear several radio and television news commentators. Are they independent sources according to the definition of "independent" given in Chapter IX, "*Reaching Conclusions*"? Radio and television commentators may depend heavily on certain large newspapers for much of their information. Newspapers may depend on one or two news information services. In a sense, news reporting becomes repetitive. You may suspect copying of information and sharing of the same material. However, this is not what helps us to understand what is happening in our world.

These sources of information should be subject to the same kind of external and internal criticism and evaluation that was explained in Chapter VIII, "*Historical Criticism*." If the central news services are providing simultaneous information for television and radio as well as for the press, how are they independent sources of information? There may be no examples of disagreement if each source is wording its material as the others do. When information is handled in such a manner, there is bound to be editing of information.

The problem of editing also leads to the question of selectivity. How much selectivity of material, whether primary or secondary, goes on before news is given out to the press or to a news broadcaster? How much do histories of local, national, regional, cultural biases or prejudices affect the judgment of those who control the news services? How much have their points of view determined what news they will present? Why will they report one story and not another?

Come back to one of the central problems involving historical processes and current news. Who are the actual eye and ear witnesses? Have people working for the major news services examined carefully the credibility and reliability of these witnesses? How much are their testimonies of current happenings slanted toward a particular cultural, economic, or political viewpoint? Are these sources the best that are available? How much of the news that is selected and given out is based on fact, probability, possibility, or uncertainty?

Think how difficult it is to examine recent events in world affairs. With regard to political stories in the news, foreign governments may edit the news before the public receives it so that they may protect themselves against unfavorable criticism. They may stifle and censor primary and secondary sources of information that are offensive to their countries' international images. Some form of censorship is practiced in every country. It is, therefore, likely that by the time you receive the news it will have been edited by a government, its central news agencies, editors of the newspapers, broadcasting companies, and the writers of the news stories. There is always the basic problem of how to tell the news in some interesting manner which will appeal to the public. The final story may include much of what the public would like to hear. Not only is the problem of editing involved, but there is the likelihood of distortions, slanted views, and, perhaps, lies.

A government may refuse to allow foreign reporters to come into its country to write freely about what is happening inside. In such a case, the news that is given out is greatly controlled and edited. It becomes difficult for other governments to test for credibility or reliability of the information that is given to them. The information may be official. That is, it bears the signatures of officials in that country. That type of primary source was discussed in Chapter VI, "*The Primary Source.*" Although primary, it could be completely unreliable evidence. In that case, your local news reporter has no direct way of writing authoritatively about the happenings in such a country. Now, multiply this form of censorship or official editing by the number of countries which still do not permit free access to sources of information.

Have you or your friends ever seen your names in any newspaper? For what reason? Suppose, you are all mentioned in the press, on the radio, and on television. Are these sources telling the truth as you know it? Did you say those things? Did you and your friends do those things? How much is actually made up for the benefit of the public? Have you been misquoted or misunderstood by reporters? Have they been fair and impartial in their reporting? How much of the actual story has been altered, censored, quieted down, or, for that matter, blown out of proportion? By whom and why?

Let us continue with the news about you and your friends. Consider the role that the reporter played as he or she gathered information about your story. Remember that the reporter was one witness. That is, if he or she was an observer at the time you were making news. It is important to know if the reporter was at the scene of action. Most of the time, the reporter is writing after the event has occurred. The reporter may have arrived too late. The reader may not be aware of this and may have the mistaken impression that the news reporter was the chief eye and/or ear witness.

Furthermore, if the reporter had been an actual witness, remember that, like all other human beings, he or she may have been subject to the same problems of loss of memory on specific points and confusion of details. The reporter may have seen what he or she wanted to see and believed what he or she wanted to believe. The individual may have allowed emotions to rule thinking and judgment.  If the reporter liked you, he or she may have slanted the account of what happened for your benefit.  If he or she harbored some grudge, you would have read about it later, much to you anger and resentment.

When the final decisions of printing took place, the size, shape, location, as well as available space for the story about you may have interfered with the reporter's written copy. Parts may have had to be left out, and content may have had to be changed, especially if the report was condensed.  People may have been anxious to have on-the-spot news coverage which was not as reliable as later reports which included some test for credibility of eye and ear witnesses.  The text may have been altered in later editions as more information became available.

Will that story about you and your friends have sold to the general public?  News writers and broadcasters may well understand the historical processes when they report the news or interpret it, but they may purposely appeal to the feelings and emotions of the public.  What the reader or listener wants to hear may be far from the reality of the situation.  An unbiased account of what you did or did not do may cause the public to lose interest in the writer and story.  If this happens, the selling point is threatened, but they are talking and writing about you.  You have a personal stake in what is being said, and so do millions of other people across the globe whose lives and recent activities are at this very moment being written and talked about.

# CHAPTER XIV

## STATISTICS

You live in a world of numbers, of sums, of totals, of amounts, in short: in a world of "statistics." When you were born, you were classified a statistic. When you entered school, you became another statistic. You became the "nth" person to be born, the "nth" person to attend school, the "nth" person in your state and nation.

Regarding processes of history, there are hundreds of thousands of questions related to historical statistics. For example, how many soldiers died in a certain battle? How many were lost or captured? How many surrendered to the enemy? How many are still alive? How many school dropouts are there? Where are they located? What are their ages? How many school dropouts have found work in the last month or in the last two months? We may ask a simple question in daily conversation about numbers of people, places, things, or public opinions. Suddenly, we have a historical statistical study.

From the standpoint of historical methodology, it is extremely important for the historian to use the same approach in gathering and analyzing statistical information as has been described in  previous chapters. The investigator should consider such questions as: How was the total obtained? Did someone take a count? Who? When? Where? Why? What information is available about the person or persons who gathered the statistics? Did the compiler rely on primary or secondary sources? Was the person who counted the number a primary source to the event? What does historical criticism reveal about the nature of the statistics? What is the range between fact and uncertainty for the final mathematical answer?

If we wish to obtain statistical information about opinions or beliefs, how do we secure it? Should we interview every person in the United States? We could select a smaller number of people, a population from various parts of our nation to represent us. In statistical analysis, we use the term "representative sample" to mean a limited number of persons, places, beliefs, and opinions, which stand for, are the same as, and therefore represent the larger number that is physically impossible to gather and analyze. When we are not able to count all the people in our nation, we must rely on a representative sample. By creating a representative sampling of the population by name and address, we survey this population. By choosing from the sample those persons to whom we wish to mail questionnaires, we collect the data from respondents who, hopefully, have mailed back the completed questionnaires.

When analyzing a representative sample, we need to consider the weighting process that was composed by the statistician.  By the term, "weighting process," is meant the process by which the number of people selected from the general public to participate in the sample closely resembles the actual percentage of that selected group within the larger (general) population. The number selected has no meaning until we attach a category to the selected population for the sample.  Consider the following categories for study:  age, sex, family income, geographic location (s) race, religion, etc.  Suppose the statistician is interested in studying the percentage of the general public who approve or disapprove of Medicare.  To develop a weighted sample of public opinion, the statistician must ascertain the percentages of people 65 and over and under the age of 65. Before accepting these percentages we must know how they were obtained.

In one location the general public consists mainly of retirees. In another section of the city, state, or region, the majority of the voting public may be under the age of 65. The statistician should consider the differences in age and should be careful to give adequate weight to each group in the representative sample. If 60% of a given population consists of voters 65 years and older, then 6 out of 10 citizens selected to be interviewed or questioned should be 65 and older. It may be necessary for accuracy to further refine the population under the age of 65. Those citizens between 18 and 45 may not be interested in Medicare and may resent having to pay taxes to support the program. Those between 46 and 64 may be thinking of retirement and may support Medicare. What percentages of those additional age groups should be questioned or interviewed? Remember, in the final study, the investigator should explain fully and carefully how the percentages of the various groups were obtained.

What is most important to understand about the representative sample is that a study of people from one section of the country, state, county, city or town may or may not reflect the thoughts, attitudes, and feelings of a population from another section. To be truly representative, the sample should be of individuals who live in the same kind of community. In your case, they should have the same financial, social, and cultural background as you. Otherwise, you may say that the findings in the sample do not reflect your opinions. However, if a national cross section of public opinion is sampled, it means that someone wants to know what the general public believes.

In theory, a cross-sectional statistical survey or questionnaire should contain responses within the study that reflect your beliefs or attitudes. In practice, the study may be composed of a sample of only urban or suburban views. It may be a cross section of views from the North, the South, or the West. To be truly a national representation, the sample should include responses from all parts of our country.

Whenever we compose a statistical study, we must be very careful to define our terms. A word such as "teenager" must be accurately defined. What does one mean by the word? What do you mean by it? Are we using the same definition? The dictionary defines a teenager as a person who is between thirteen and nineteen years of age. Do you notice any problems now? The sample may heavily represent the sixteen to eighteen year old category. It may ignore the thirteen through fifteen and nineteen year old age groups. What about twenty-year-olds? Perhaps, a data collector may include the latter age group in a survey.

By now, you should realize that it may be impossible to gather information on every single individual or every single item. Therefore, many of the numbers that you read in texts are not complete totals but are totals taken from samples. Writers should state that these numbers are only approximations or that they have been arrived at by taking the answers from representative samples and multiplying those answers by the number of neighborhoods, schools, businesses, farms, etc., studied in the selected localities. How accurate is the arithmetic? Too often, we are forced to memorize a certain number. But do we stop to consider the accuracy of that sum, total, or amount? Perhaps, we are afraid to question the given answer. You may think, "Who am I to question a number or historical statistic found on page twenty-two of the history text?" Of course, you understand from previous discussion that you have every right to question the evidence externally and internally and so should the writer.

Let us turn to some additional problems in historical statistical analysis. Suppose you are examining the total number of pounds of any item that had sold during a particular time in American history. Some scales may have been or are defective. Waste products may have been or are included in the total weight. In the case of cotton production in the South prior to the Civil War: Was there a standard size for a bale of cotton? Were waste products gathered up in those bales? After the cleansing process did take place, how much pure cotton was actually produced? Did those who noted the statistics discover if waste products were included in the totals given to them? Was false information purposely given? If so, why?

In some cases, historical statistics which are considered official are not reliable. If you were to trace the source of a number or total given in a governmental or associational record, you would, perhaps, find that the person responsible for collecting these statistics was not even mentioned by name in the document. How did the data collector obtain these figures? Did he or she personally interview responsible leaders of organizations? Did the data collector send out questionnaires? Were all the questionnaires filled out properly; were they filled out honestly?

Money value in dollars and cents or in foreign currency runs the risk of being so complicated to figure that it may be the easy way out to state some figure that looks impressive. Levels of income go up and down; so does the cost of living or the cost of production and distribution of products and services. It is extremely difficult to convert the money costs of yesterday into modern or up-to-date figures. Think, for example, how difficult it is to determine the present day money value of tobacco sent from America to England in any year prior to 1775. Yet, some authors write with such authority that one would think that they had spent their entire lives doing nothing but determining the monetary value of tobacco in the American colonies.

Historical statistics for any number of human beings involved in an event and series of events are always difficult to quantify accurately. We run the risk of damage to records, loss of vital information, as well as exaggeration, or understatement. Were those who took the count accurate? Who knows? Were they careful in their work or so sloppy that they made careless mistakes when they made their final reports? Did they take samples or count every person? How many people whom they interviewed lied for reasons of their own? Was it embarrassment, loyalty to a friend, country, community, or cowardice, revenge, hate?

Finally, returning to you, are you willing to answer personal questions for surveys about political, economic, or social matters? You may fear losing a job, friends, or influence. However, your responses, whether or not they represent your honest beliefs, are tallied along with other people's answers. Historians will be quoting these replies. They will say that you believe thus and so, when perhaps you really do not. Only you know if you are honest in your replies. And it will be up to you to evaluate the truthfulness of others when you involve yourself in the world of historical statistical analysis.

# FOR FURTHER STUDY

Ask your family or friends if they ever answered questions for a survey. What was the purpose of the survey? What were the kinds of questions which were asked?

Think about the purposes of surveys and questionnaires. Are they being taken for political, economic, or cultural reasons? How do you think answers that you give will be used? How should they be used?

Find a local newspaper article which bases its "facts" on a survey. Ask the newspaper editor for a copy of the survey. Read it carefully. Do you find any questions that may be interpreted more than one way? Are there any questions which you think some people would not answer honestly? Why not?

Discuss with a statistician how to create a "random" sample based upon a representative population.

The following excerpt is from an article written by Jim Rutenberg and Megan C. Thee in The New York Times, dated July 27, 2006. What questions come to your mind as you read the following insert, entitled, "How the Poll Was Conducted." The title of the article is, "Poll Shows Growing Skepticism in U.S. Over Peace in the Middle East."

> The latest New York Times/CBS News poll is based on telephone interviews conducted July 21 through July 25 with 1,127 adults throughout the United States.
>
> The sample of telephone exchanges called was randomly selected by a computer from a complete list of more than 42,000 active residential exchanges across the country.
>
> Within each exchange, random digits were added to form a complete telephone number, thus permitting access to listed and unlisted numbers alike. Within each household, one adult was designated by a random procedure to be the respondent for the survey.
>
> The results have been weighted to take account of household size and number of telephone lines into the residence and to adjust for variation in the sample relating to geographic region, sex, race, marital status, age and education.
>
> In theory, in 19 cases out of 20, over all results based on such samples will differ by no more then three percentage points in · either direction from what would have been obtained by seeking

out all American adults. For smaller subgroups, the margin of sampling error is larger. Shifts in results between polls also have a larger sampling error.

In addition to sampling error, the practical difficulties of conducting any survey of public opinion may introduce other sources of error into the poll. Variation in the wording and order of questions, for example, may lead to somewhat different results.

Dr. Michael R. Kagay of Princeton, N.J., assisted <u>The Times</u> in its polling analysis. Complete questions and results are available at nytimes.com/polls.

By permission of<br>
<u>The New York Times</u>

If you are interested in studying mathematical, and by extension, historical statistics, why not compare samples? Examine their compositions. Each sample should be composed of a population from within the same or similar geographic area. All variables or factors selected for inclusion as well as their weighting formulations should be the same or similar. Observe the final averages given for goods and services as well as opinions and beliefs. Analyze numeric variations and, especially, the reasons for those variations between and among sample conclusions.

Coal Production in Pennsylvania for the Years 1880-1900,
Ten-Year Intervals:  Graph and Discussion




Jack Block
The Study of History
Dr. E. Hunt
Columbia University

## PREFACE

This paper has three parts. Part one deals with a definition of coal and the problem of studying its production.

Part two gives the statistics available for coal production in the years 1880, 1890, and 1900. Primary and secondary sources are compared in order to bring a reasonable conclusion to this section.

The third part consists of a graph which summarizes the findings of part two.

# I

"Coal" may be defined as a black or dark brown combustible substance consisting of carbonized vegetable matter and is used as fuel.[1] Coal is divided into three types depending upon the amount of carbon it contains. Anthracite, or hard coal, has the most carbon. Bituminous, or soft coal, has lower carbon content than anthracite. Lignite, the softest coal, is brown in color and has the lowest amount of carbon.[2]

Five major problems result from a study of coal and its production. The first concerns lignite. Statistics are available for bituminous and anthracite coal. No sources examined mention lignite production for the years 1880, 1890, or 1900. Thus, the total of anthracite and bituminous coal will then have to stand for the total of coal produced in any year.

The second problem stems from the word, "production." Most sources do not explain what is meant by production. Only two define the term. They state that coal taken from the mine includes: coal shipped out of the city, coal used by the mining town itself, coal used to heat the mining building, and coal used by the miners for home consumption.[3] In this paper, coal production will mean the total of the above items.

The third problem relates to the term used to measure production. The word, "ton," has been used in all the sources studied. However, the word does not stand by itself. "Long," "short," "net," and "gross" are added to describe the exact weight in pounds for each ton. A long ton consists of two thousand two hundred forty (2,240) pounds of coal, a short ton, two thousand pounds (2,000).[4] A gross ton and a net ton are the same as a short ton.[5]

The long ton is exactly two hundred forty (240) pounds heavier than the short ton, or 12% greater than each short ton. On the other hand, the number of carloads, or containers of short tons produced is exactly 12% larger then the number of carloads, or containers of long tons. Thus, the total production of short tons is equal to the total of longs tons.[6] In this paper all statistics will be in short tons in order to simplify the study of the data.

The fourth problem exists because no figures are available to show the waste matter for each ton produced. Perhaps, it was computed and subtracted from the total, perhaps, not. This problem may help to explain why there is a difference in the two sets of statistics presented in part two.

---

[1] Homer Green, Coal and the Coal Mines (Boston: Houghton Mifflin Company, 1928), p.7.
[2] Loc.cit.
[3] Report on Mineral Industries in the United States at the Eleventh Census: 1890, U.S. Department of the Interior (Washington: 1892), p.400.
 Mineral Resources of the U.S.A. Calendar Year 1901, U.S. Department of the Interior, Geological Survey (Washington: 1902), p.428.
[4] Ibid., p. 281.
[5] Clarence L.Barnhart, ed The American College Dictionary (New York: Random House, 1947), p.534, p.816.
[6] Howard N. Eavenson, The First Century and a Quarter of American Coal Industry (Pittsburgh: Kuppers Building, 1942), pp. 11-12.

The last problem is the most important of all. The statistics are official for the State of Pennsylvania and for the various bureaus of the United States Government. But, they do not show the actual amounts in tons reported by each entrepreneur, or each mining unit.

From where does the state of Pennsylvania or the United States Government receive its information for the years 1880, 1890 and 1900? Only one source actually lists the agencies responsible for statistical reports. The Historical Statistics of the United States quotes the work, Mineral Resources of the United States. However, it fails to analyze the data.[7] There is no proof presented in any of these or other works examined that verifies that double, or triple, or multiple counting of tons did not occur. This last problem and the other four will be further discussed in the next section, part two.

## II

Recently, this writer wrote to the Bureau of Mines, Pennsylvania, for statistics on coal production. He received the following figures.[8]

| Year | Type | Production | Combined Total |
|------|------|-----------|----------------|
| 1880 | Anthracite | 27,974,532 | 44,538,972 |
|      | Bituminous | 16,564,440 | |
| 1890 | Anthracite | 44,986,286 | 85,870,389 |
|      | Bituminous | 40,884,103 | |
| 1900 | Anthracite | 57,363,396 | 136,681,758 |
|      | Bituminous | 79,318,362 | |

(Short tons)

It was clear from these figures that by 1900 bituminous coal production overtook anthracite. In fact, all sources used for this paper indicated the same trend.[9] The reason for this change was that the demand for the cheaper, soft coal became great when industry began to use the bituminous coal. Household fuel was still supplied by anthracite. Interestingly, the construction of large office buildings and apartment houses with great needs for heat and hot water made the use of anthracite coal expensive and impractical.[10]

Mr. Higgins has not documented any of the above figures nor does he reveal his sources of information. However, this writer does find some agreement with those of Mr. Frank Hall,

---

[7] Mineral Resources of the U.S.A. Calendar Year 1883, U.S. Department of the Interior, Geological Surrey (Washington: 1884), p. 11, as quoted by Historical Statistics of the U.S.A. 1789-1945, U. S. Department of the Interior (Washington: 1949), p. 133.
[8] Information obtained in correspondence with Mr. John F. Higgins.
[9] All sources show this increase in 1900.
[10] Mineral Resources of the U.S.A. for Calendar Year 1901, U.S. Department of the Interior, Geological Survey (Washington: 1902), p. 416.

Chief of Mines, and Mining, Pennsylvania. His office gives amounts only for the years 1880 and 1900.[11]

| Year | Type | Production | Combined Total |
|------|------|-----------|----------------|
| 1880 | Anthracite | 31,331,476 | 47,895,916 |
|      | Bituminous | 16,564,440 | |
| 1900 | Anthracite | 57,363,396 | 136,681,758 |
|      | Bituminous | 79,318,362 | |

(Net tons)

The only difference in statistics is for anthracite production in 1880. 3,356,944 more tons are recorded by Mr. Hall than by Mr. Higgins. There is a mistake, however, that this writer found in Mr. Hall's numbers. They are all converted to net, or short ton numbers. If one uses the formula expressed in part one of this paper and multiplies 27,974,532, the figure given by Mr. Higgins, by 1.12 or by 12%, the answer comes to 31,331,475.84 or simply, 31,331,476 short tons, Mr. Hall's answer. The mistake is that Mr. Hall multiplied by 24% instead of 12%. By adding the difference he was adding the extra 12%. Therefore, by correcting this error, this writer finds that Mr. Hall and Mr. Higgins completely agree.

The last source in this first set of statistics, set A, comes again from the Department of Mines, Pennsylvania, for the year 1955. The following amounts are recorded for bituminous coal production for 1880, 1890 and 1900[12]

| Year | Type | Production |
|------|------|-----------|
| 1880 | Bituminous | 16,564,440 |
| 1890 | Bituminous | 40,784,003 |
| 1900 | Bituminous | 79,318,362 |

(Net tons)

There is a difference of 100,000 short tons for the year 1890. This writer offers no reason for this difference.

The second set of sources, set B, generally agrees with each other, and interestingly, are all greater than the totals of set A. Also, set B may be traced back to records of 1882. The earliest

[11] Mines and Mining in Pennsylvania, by Frank Hall, Pennsylvania Department of Mines and Mining (Harrisburg: J.J. Kuhn, 1919), p.10.
[12] History of Pennsylvania Bituminous Coal, Pennsylvania Department of Mines and Mining (1955), p. 59.

source is the Geological Survey by the Department of the Interior, of the United States.[13] The survey records the following:

| Year | Type | Production | Combined Total |
|------|------|------------|----------------|
| 1880 | Anthracite | 28,649,812 | 47,047,975 |
|      | Bituminous | 18,425,163 |                |

The Census of 1890 agrees with the above totals.[14] However, it is possible that the Census Bureau copied these amounts given by the Geological Survey.[15]

The first complete listing of amounts available for coal for the years 1880, 1890, and 1900 were found in a work put out by the United States Department of the Interior in 1901. The figures given were the following:[16]

| Year | Type | Production | Combined Total |
|------|------|------------|----------------|
| 1880 | Anthracite | 28,649,812 | 47,074,975 |
|      | Bituminous | 18,425,163 |                |
| 1890 | Anthracite | 46,468,641 | 88,770,814 |
|      | Bituminous | 42,302,173 |                |
| 1900 | Anthracite | 57,367,915 | 137,210,241 |
|      | Bituminous | 79,842,326 |                |

(Short tons)

In 1902, the United States Census came out with its figures and gave the same totals as those recorded above.[17] In fact, the Census gave credit to Mineral Resource, from which it quoted the statistics.[18] By 1949, three more studies of coal production were made which gave credit to the statistics given above by the Department of Interior in 1901.[19]

---

[13] Mineral Resources of the U.S.A. for the Calendar Year 1882, U.S. Department of the Interior, Geological Survey (Washington: 1883), p.7.

[14] Report on the Mineral Industries in the United States at the Eleventh Census: 1890, U.S. Department of the Interior (Washington: 1892), p.346.

[15] Ibid., p. 400.

[16] Mineral Resources of the U.S.A. for Calendar Year 1901, p. 354.

[17] Special Reports: Mines and Quarries 1902, U.S. Department of Commerce and Labor, Bureau of the Census (Washington: 1905), pp. 293, 295.

[18] Loc.cit.

[19] The Mineral Production of Pennsylvania 1911, Pennsylvania Topographic and Geological Survey Commission (Harrisburg:The Telegraph Printing Company 1911), p.9.
Pennsylvania's Mineral Heritage, Pennsylvania Department of Internal Affairs (Harrisburg: 1944), pp.9, 13, 14.
Historical Statistics of the U.S.A. 1789-1945, A Supplement to the Statistical Abstract of the U.S.A., US Department of the Interior (Washington: 1949), p. 142.

The Statistical Abstract Supplement revealed evidence obtained from Mineral Resources, written in 1883. The quotation explained how the statistical information was obtained.[20] It stated that sources used were reports of agents, and correspondents of the Department of the Interior, "...the transportation records of the railroad companies, report of the state mines inspectors, and the State Geological Survey, etc."[21] Statistical Abstract further explained that since 1890, coal production figures were compiled on the basis of annual reports published by the coal producers themselves.[22]

What may be said about the two sets of statistics, sets A and B, found in this paper? When the totals for both sets are compared, it is found that there is a difference of over two million short tons, for 1880 and 1890. For 1900, the difference has dropped to over one half million short tons.

This writer offers several possible reasons for the differences. The first is suggested by Mr. Howard Eavenson. In his book on coal production, Mr. Eavenson explains that coal production reports before 1885 were few and not reasonably accurate.[23] Perhaps, this answer explains why there is a lower difference found for 1900. Unfortunately, Mr. Eavenson does not document this statement regarding the earlier inaccuracies.

The second reason may be that statistics gathered for set A do not consider waste matter, rock, water, and dirt, which add weight to the mined coal. Nothing is stated in either set that waste matter was removed prior to calculation.

Multiple counting is the third reason offered. It may be that reports sent in simultaneously by railroad companies, mining companies and inspectors were combined. This would increase the total and account for the higher figures in set B.

The fourth reason seems the most unlikely; but, it should be mentioned. Perhaps, the mining company reports overestimated their totals. However, this is unlikely because 1880-1900 was a period in economic history when labor was fighting frantically for pay increases. If the company were to report large annual production figures, the miners could very well use these figures to their advantage. Greater productivity called for higher wages. The company would rather underestimate the production figures in its reports.

The fifth and last reason may be that errors were made in either set A or set B. In the Census of 1902, there is a statement which explains the complexity of getting totals for coal production during any year. Some state reports cover the fiscal year ending June 30.[24] But, the Mine Inspectors' reports cover the year ending December 31.[25] The Census Report covers the

---

[20] See Footnote 7.
[21] Loc.cit.
[22] Loc.cit.
[23] Howard N. Eavenson, The First Century and a Quarter of American Coal Industry (Pittsburgh: Kuppers Building, 1942), pp. 1, 11, 12.
[24] Special Reports: Mines and Quarries, 1902, U.S. Department of Commerce and Labor, Bureau of the Census (Washington: 1905), p. 131.
[25] Loc.cit.

year ending December 31.[26]   With such complexity, either Set A or set B may contain miscalculations.

The only conclusion this writer draws, in view of the evidence available for this paper, is uncertainty that either set A or set B represents the production of anthracite and bituminous coal for the State of Pennsylvania in years 1880, 1890, and 1900.

### III

Total Production for Anthracite and Bituminous Coal in the State of Pennsylvania for the Years 1880, 1890, and 1900 Showing Differences of Calculations, according to government reports, and recorded in millions of short tons.

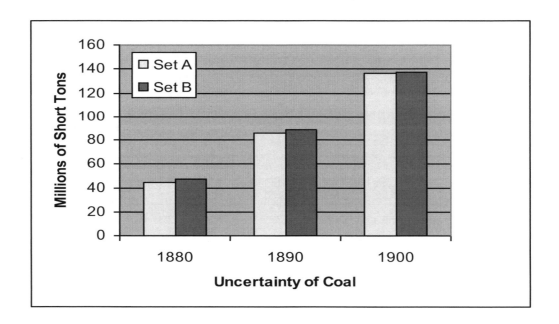

---

[26] Loc.cit.

# Bibliography

## Primary Sources

Pennsylvania. Department of Internal Affairs, Bureau of Statistics. <u>Pennsylvania's Mineral Heritage</u>. Harrisburg: 1944. 240 pp.

Pennsylvania. Department of Mines and Mining. <u>History of Pennsylvania Bituminous Coal</u>, 1955. 65 pp.

Pennsylvania. Department of Mines and Mining. <u>Mines and Mining In Pennsylvania</u>, by Frank Hall. Harrisburg: J.J. Kuhn, 1919. 26 pp.

Pennsylvania. Topographic and Geological Survey Commission. <u>The Mineral Production of Pennsylvania, 1911</u>. Harrisburg: The Telegraph Printing Company, 1911. 84 pp.

U.S. Department of Commerce, Bureau of the Census. <u>Historical Statistics of the U.S. 1789-1945</u>. Washington: 1949. 363 pp.

U.S. Department of Commerce and Labor, Bureau of the Census. <u>Special Reports 1902 Mines and Quarries</u>. Washington: 1905, 1123 pp.

U.S. Department of the Interior, Geological Survey. <u>Mineral Resources of the U.S.A.</u>, Washington: 1883, 813 pp.

U.S. Department of the Interior, Census Office. <u>Report on Mineral Industries in the U.S.A. at the Eleventh Census, 1890</u>. Washington: 1892. 858 pp.

U.S. Department of the Interior, Census Office. <u>Production of Bituminous Coal</u>. Washington: 1882. 9 pp.

U.S. Department of the Interior, Geological Survey. <u>Mineral Resources of the U.S.A.</u>, Calendar Year 1901. Washington: 1902. 996 pp.

**Secondary Sources**

Eavenson, Howard N. <u>The First Century and a Quarter of American Coal Industry</u>. Pittsburgh: Kuppers Builiding, 1942. 600 pp.
   This is a clear and valuable book for a history of coal and its production.

Greene, Homer. <u>Coal and the Coal Mines</u>. Boston: Houghton Miflin Company, 1928. 225 pp.
   This is not as complete as Mr. Eavenson's work, but it does describe types of coal well.

Higgins, John F., Letter to Jack Block, dated July 10, 1959.

Moore, Elwood S. <u>Coal: Its Properties, Analysis, Classification, Geology, Extraction, Uses and Distribution</u>. New York: John Wiley and Sons, Inc., 1922. 462 pp.

Shurick, A.T. <u>The Coal Industry</u>. Boston: Little, Brown and Company 1924. 383 pp.
   This work is not as complete as Mr. Eavenson's.

# CHAPTER XV

# CHRONOLOGY

What is today's date? If we say that today is September 6, 200_, we make several assumptions. First, we assume that today is September 6, 200_. Second, we assume that everyone agrees that this is the date. We in the United States agree, but we should not expect the entire world to accept our calendar. Third, we assume that there are no errors in our past calendar calculations. Finally, we assume that happenings on this day will be recorded somewhere by somebody so that future generations will have a record of past events.

An important task for the historian is to place an event or series of events as accurately as possible within a certain time frame. Unfortunately, historical methodology has no magic formula that will date all events according to one world-wide calendar. So many calendars exist that it is difficult to base every happening on just one. For example, we use a Christian, Western European calendar. But we must also consider the Chinese, Japanese-Oriental calendars. Do not forget Hebraic, Moslem, Roman, and Greek calendars. Consider those non-Western societies which still date their events according to their own special calendars.

Remember the national pride that all peoples have. As a citizen, you are rightfully proud of your country and of its heritage. But you must be open-minded enough to realize that people in other parts of the world feel just as strongly about their culture and traditions. They have been brought up to respect their country's record in world history. Whereas, we think of our country as a few hundred years old, they may regard their culture or way of life as thousands of years old.

At this very moment, there are scores of historians and students from many different lands who are studying primary and secondary sources. Suppose a certain critical analyst in a distant land is analyzing records of his or her nation's history. The analyst must absolutely ignore our Western calendar and must concentrate on the problem of dating events according to the nation's calendar. It is ridiculous, don't you think, for a Chinese scholar to refer to some event as having taken place on September 6, 200_? The history of his or her native land has been continuous for several thousand years.

Consider how foolish it sounds when we speak of ancient history, of the Middle Ages, or of modern history. Consider the relative importance of each of these terms: the Middle of what? Ancient compared to another country's point of view? What is Ancient? The scholar in China must examine the contact that scholar's country has had with all nations, Western and non-Western. Because of these contacts, controversies may have developed regarding the time when a particular event or a series of events occurred. According to a treaty signed by two nations, one of which may be China, the date placed at the bottom of the treaty becomes important in determining chronology.

In historical methodology, "chronology" is the study of events from their beginning to their end. The study includes the dating of these events. Whatever date we affix to an event should be, in theory, the actual date. You are already aware, however, of mistakes in records indicating that an external error was made. How often are we in such a hurry that we date letters, checks, documents, or certificates incorrectly?

Have you ever wondered how peoples around the globe recall their past? On what basis have they determined their calendars? The word "<u>year</u>" does not have the same meaning to all peoples. In one culture, the term will apply to the lunar month. The new moon will signify the start of a new year. To another culture, the word "<u>generation</u>" will not mean the total of twenty-five years, but it will stand for a year. So, birthdays have been recorded, as well as thousands of other occurrences, during a certain generation.

Eyewitness accounts may reveal phrases such as, "the year of the flood," "the year of the rich harvest," "the year of the great hunt," "the year of the great famine." Secondary sources may use expressions such as, "in the days of the flood," "many generations ago," "in the generation of," or "many moons ago". We say, "many years ago." We assume that other cultures are counting the number of days it takes for the earth to completely revolve around the sun. It makes as much sense to count as a year the number of days it takes for a full moon to appear, for winter to begin and end, or for spring to start and finish. Who is to say which way is the best?

Do you see how complicated it becomes when we want to calculate when an event in world history occurred? Who is to say which calendar is the official or the ideal one to use? Take, for example, the journey of Marco Polo to China. When Marco Polo left for the Orient, what year was it according to the Western Christian calendar? When he finally arrived in the Orient, what year was it according to the Chinese calendar?

Finally, we must become aware of how all peoples around the globe borrow from each other ideas, habits, and inventions. In the United States, we have spoken of the "generation gap" and of the "now generation." Do you notice that the concept of generation becomes more important than our traditional yearly record? We are borrowing from other societies when we pay tribute to the word, "generation." Imagine what historians of the future will think when they come to analyze the records of the "now" generation!

This is what makes the study and writing of history exciting: The fact that you are living now and what counts now, this year, this minute, this generation is what matters to you. It sounds rather humorous when you think how puzzled the historian of the future will be when he or she wonders what a flower in the "flower generation" meant. "What did the writers of that earlier "day" have in mind?" one will ask. Remember that each society has its own special way of treating the chronology of its history. And before we laugh at others, we should take an insightful look at ourselves.

# FOR FURTHER STUDY

Try to discover what was taking place during a given year in all parts of the world.

Discuss the meaning of the following:

> The Victorian Age
> The Kennedy Years
> The Ming Dynasty

When was George Washington born? Why was his birth date changed within his own lifetime? How may the new laws about Mondays for National Holidays further change our concept of famous birth dates?

What dates will be used as we move space ships out of our galaxy? Shall we continue to use "earth years" or another planet's years?

When and Where Was the First Public High School Established
Within The State of New York?

Jack Block
The Study of History
Dr. E. Hunt
Columbia University

# Preface

A problem exists because there has been no standard meaning in use to apply to the phrase, "high school." At times it has been called "academic," "union", or "secondary" school. No proof is submitted to show that these words are definitely synonymous.

The Lockport school system used the words, "union school." When New York State authorized the establishment of the Lockport Union School, the act stated that the school would be used by those students who wanted to learn the higher branches of education. In the case of the New York Free Academy, the act authorizing its establishment mentioned that this school was to be used by persons who had been pupils of the common schools of New York City. Palmyra Union School's usage of the word "union" could not be defined since sources did not explain the term, "union school," in any way.

The term, "high school," today, means a school beyond the elementary, or primary grades (grades one through eight), which is open to students who have completed these grades. The length of high school study is normally four years. Although there are technical, academic, and comprehensive high schools at the present time, one may guess that only academic subjects were taught in the early high schools before the 1850's. The need for technical schools was not essential until the Civil War era.

Even if one eliminates the vocational or technical high school, it is still difficult to adequately compare these early high schools because of a lack of evidence concerning the curriculum of each school. Lockport Union describes its subjects as "advanced departments." The New York Free Academy curriculum is unavailable and the reference for Palmyra Union School is lacking in this respect. None of the three schools studied is examined with regard to the duration of high school education. The evidence examined does not state the number of years required to complete a high school education. Even though "junior" high schools are prevalent in the United States today, this study does not include them. The reason is that nowhere in the available primary or secondary sources of early 19th century educational literature does the word, "junior" appear.

As for the word, "public," a public high school must be publicly controlled, supported, and without any charge of tuition. Whether or not a school is called by the name "public high school", "free academy," "union school," or "free high school," it has to meet the definition given above.

In conclusion, this writer has arbitrarily defined the word, "established," as the day a school first opened.

In the year 1849, the Free School Act of New York State was passed.[1] This act gave legal authority for any community in New York State to establish its own public school system. Before this act was approved by the state legislature, individual communities had already established their own free schools.[2] They had each decided that children were entitled to a free, public school education. However, they generally considered only elementary school education free for all children.

Three communities had established secondary schools which were completely or primarily public by 1849. These communities were by name Palmyra, Lockport, and New York City. The schools established were in turn called Palmyra Union School, Lockport Union School, and New York Free Academy. Each of these schools, at one time or another, was said to be the first public high school.

It is this writer's opinion that Palmyra Union may possibly be the first pubic high school established in the State of New York. Only two sources are available which date the establishment of Palmyra Union School. They are both secondary accounts and therefore do not provide certainty, or even probability, of evidence. The first source comes from the writing of Thomas L. Cook, the second from Alexis Muller, Jr.

Cook, in his work, explains that during 1847 a new union free school was built and occupied by 1848 in Palmyra. He even lists the names of the teachers as well as those of the students attending the school.[3] Nothing more is mentioned about the school's beginning, nor is there any reference to document his statements. Cook explains in his preface that he is only interested in telling the history of his town for the enjoyment of his readers and says that he is not concerned with the historian's task. Thus, one cannot be sure of the reliability of his evidence.

The remaining evidence is taken from Mr. Muller's historical report on the development of the public school system in Lockport, New York. He writes that there "were reports" that Palmyra was following a plan similar to the union school movement of Lockport. He goes on to say that Palmyra actually succeeded in opening its union school at an earlier date than did Lockport.[4] Unfortunately, Mr. Muller does not document his statements. Therefore, by taking the two sources one may establish a possibility that Palmyra Union School, in 1848, was the first public high school.

What is most interesting about Mr. Muller's evidence is that it refutes the work of two researchers who have independently claimed that Lockport Union School was the first public high school in the State of New York. Furthermore, Mr. Muller has written on behalf of the Lockport Board of Education, a brief history of Lockport's school system. He seems to have purposely placed his evidence of Palmyra into his findings on Lockport's Union School. Perhaps, he is directing his remarks to Paul Monroe and John Gifford. They are the two men

---

[1]New York State Statutes (1849), "An Act Establishing Free Schools Throughout the State" (Troy: A. W. Scribner and A. West), Chap. 140, p. 193.

[2]Samuel Sidwell Randall, History of the Common School System of New York (New York: Ivison, Blakeman·and Taylor Company, 1871), p. 287. Randall does not state his sources of information.

[3]Thomas L. Cook, Palmyra and Vicinity (Palmyra, New York: Press of the Palmyra Courier Journal, 1930), pp. 268-269.

[4]Alexis Muller, Jr., History of the Public Schools 100 Years of Education (Lockport: Board of Education, 1947), p.23.

who have held Lockport Union School to be first. It is only natural to turn to the evidence of these men and to determine the reliability of their material.

Paul Monroe claimed that the founding of Lockport Union School and the New York Free Academy legalized the public high school system.[5] The documentation for this as well as for all statements in the text was typed by Monroe. The typed footnotes were then complied into a second work and sent by Mr. Monroe to the University of Michigan where the material was put on microfilm.

Upon checking the microfilm copy of this manuscript, this writer found a gross error. Where the footnote reference to the Lockport School was supposed to be, there was instead a reference to the New York Free Academy. Mr. Monroe had omitted any reference to the Lockport School.[6] This writer wrote to the University of Michigan and received word that Paul Monroe was responsible for the omission since the microfilm printed whatever material was on the original manuscript. The University also stated that as Mr. Monroe was no longer living, it could not change the film nor edit the material. Under these circumstances, the material which Monroe wrote about Lockport became useless since he offered no evidence for his statements concerning the Lockport Union School.

In his doctoral study, Walter John Gifford states on pages ten, fifty-seven and seventy-one, that the first public high school in New York State to be fully established was the Lockport Union School.[7] The first statement on page ten has no documentation. The second on page fifty-seven refers to the Act of New York State which gave legal permission for the village of Lockport to establish the Lockport Union School.[8]

This act, passed March 31, 1847, gave the general details for the establishment of a high school of learning for students of the Lockport school system. It stated that when these students possessed the necessary qualifications in age and learning they could go to the Union School. The act did not mention what qualifications were necessary. A tuition fee was to be charged. The act called for the building of a school, which was to be called the Lockport Union School, in which, "…shall be taught only the higher branches of education."[9]

Only in his reference on page seventy-one did Gifford actually state that Lockport Union School was the first public high school of New York to be legalized and the first to be established. He gave three sources to document his statement. One of the sources used in the footnote was from the minutes of the Board of Education of Lockport for the year 1848. As stated by Gifford,[10] and Muller,[11] these minutes for the entire year of 1848 were burned in a fire at a private dwelling in which they were being held. The fire occurred in 1850.

---

[5]Paul Monroe, Founding of the American Public School System (New York: MacMillan Company, 1940), vol. 1, p. 417.
[6]Paul Monroe, Founding of the American Public School System (Ann Arbor, Michigan: University Microfilms, 1940), vol. 2, quo.584, 587.
[7]Walter John Gifford, Historical Development of the New York State High School System (Albany: J.B. Lyon Company, 1922), pp. 10,57, 71.
[8]New York State Statutes (1847), "An Act in Relation to Common Schools in the Village of Lockport" (Albany: C.Van Benthuysen), chap. 51, pp. 54, - 57.
[9]Ibid., p. 27.
[10]Gifford, op. cit., p 71.
[11]Muller, op. cit., p. 26.

Another source used was the register of the Union School for the year 1848. However, there is no copy available except at Lockport. The contents of this register would probably reveal that day when the school officially opened. On July 5, 1848, the Lockport Union School became officially established, for on that same day the school opened for the first time.[12]

The last source for this footnote came from the Catalog of the Union School. This was also the fiftieth anniversary issue. But Gifford never mentioned what particular value this issue had for his readers.

Mr. Gifford depended upon an act of 1847 granting permission for the establishment of a public high school in Lockport. It was understandable that he should have examined this act. It was the first act, during the 1840's that specifically dealt with the establishment of a public school in the State of New York.[13] But acts alone did not establish all the schools prior to 1849. It should be understood that prior to this year when the Free School Act was passed, it was up to the individual communities to establish free systems.[14]

The reference to the Minutes of the Board of Education meetings in Lockport for the year 1848 would be impossible to secure. Gifford himself stated that they were burned. Yet, it is surprising that he would even mention them in his work. Had Mr. Gifford located other sources pertaining to the board meetings for the year 1848, they might have shed light on the development of the school.

Finally, and perhaps most important, is the provision in the Lockport Union School Act which expressly permitted a tuition fee. The act declares that, "…said board of education shall have power…to fix the rate of tuition fees in said union school…"[15]. It further states that the tuition fee is not to be greater than two dollars per quarter for residents. No tuition is required for the primary schools "…but the same shall be free schools."[16] Accordingly, the act is granting legal authority for the establishment of a non-public school.

There are two sources available which definitely state that a tuition was charged and paid by students of the Lockport Union School. These materials come from Mr. Gifford and Mr. Muller. However, they are both secondary in nature. Gifford states that tuition was charged to the students.[17] It is surprising that Mr. Gifford did not stop at this point to reconsider what he was writing. A public school must be free of tuition and yet he considers Lockport Union a public high school.

This writer wrote to Mr. Muller and inquired about the tuition charge. Mr. Muller answered that according to the records of the school, tuition was charged but that in his opinion the charge of one or two dollars was so small that students could easily afford to pay it.

---

[12]Ibid., p. 27.
[13]This writer has examined all the New York Educational Laws enacted between 1840 and 1848.
[14]Randall, op. cit., p. 287.
[15]New York State Statues (1847), "An Act in Relation to Common Schools in the Village of Lockport" (Albany: C. VanBenthyysen), chap. 51, p.54.
[16]Ibid., p. 57.
[17]Gifford, op cit., p. 57.

Moreover, the school allowed a student to work to pay for the tuition. Usually, such a student would chop wood and perform odd jobs for the school.[18]

No primary evidence is submitted to prove that Lockport Union was established as a non-public high school. Mr. Muller and Mr. Gifford agree that tuition was charged. As Mr. Muller was writing on behalf of the Board of Education of Lockport and had official access to its records, it may be assumed that his evidence was supported by sources. Therefore, it is this writer's belief that Lockport Union School was possibly not established on July 5, 1848 as a public high school.

The last of the three schools to be considered is the New York Free Academy which opened and was established in January, 1849.[19] Primary sources are lacking to prove that this school was established as a high school.

The act granting legal establishment for the Free Academy was passed on May 7, 1847.[20] This act gave the outline for the school's development. It stated that the academy was to be under the "…supervision, management, and government of the said Board of Education."[21] More important, however, was the statement that "The Board of Education for the city…shall have the power to establish a Free Academy in the City of New York."[22]

In fact, there is substantial, primary material available to show that no tuition was charged. Two documents discovered by Mr. Monroe reveal the desired information. The first document is a work entitled, "Dissent of Horace Greelye," published by the Board of Education of New York City for the year 1850. In this dissent, Mr. Greelye does not approve of the Free Academy, and gives his reasons. He says, "I distrust and challenge the policy of giving a costly education at public expense."[23] The second document, an address given by Mr. Benedict, president of the Board of Education of the City of New York, honors the Free Academy's first anniversary. Mr. Benedict states, "This is one of the common schools, free to all."[24]

There is no substantial body of information which conflicts with the statement that the academy was free. Besides Mr. Monroe's microfilmed evidence, the secondary works of John Gifford and Elmer Brown throw further light on the problem. Mr. Brown implies that the first public high school was the Free Academy and he refers to the act of 1847 as evidence.[25] According to Mr. Gifford the Free Academy became established in 1849, just a year after the establishment of the Lockport Union School.[26]

---

[18]Information obtained in correspondence with Mr. Muller.
[19]A. Emerson Palmer, The New York Public School (New York: The MacMillan Company, 1905), p. 237.
[20]New York State Statutes (1847), "An Act authorizing the Board of Education of the City and County of New York to establish a Free Academy in said City." (Albany: C. Van Benthuysen), chap. 206. pp. 208-212.
[21]Ibid., p. 210.
[22]Ibid., p. 208.
[23]Monroe, op.cit., vol. 2, quo. 585, p. 1518.
[24]Ibid., quo. 586, p. 1520.
[25]Elmer Ellsworth Brown, The Making of Our Middle Schools (New York: Longmans, Green and Company, 1902), pp 312-313.
[26]Gifford, op.cit., p. 57.

The Free Academy was erected at the corner of Lexington Avenue and Twenty-Third Street, Manhattan, New York. Both Mr. French[27] and Mr. Wilson[28] agree on the exact location of the school. Mr. French further states that the building is like "…an edifice in the Gothic style of the town halls of the Netherlands, 80 by 100 feet…"[29].

There are several conclusions to be drawn from the report. One of these concerns Palmyra. Because of the lack of substantial evidence only a possibility may be reached regarding Palmyra Union's development. This school may possibly be the first public high school to be established in New York in 1848. Until further evidence is located either for or against Palmyra, it will have to stand as it is.

Regarding Lockport Union School, evidence proves that this school was possibly not originally established as a completely free high school.

Only a possibility may be reached regarding New York Free Academy since no primary source is available to prove that it was established as a public high school in January, 1848.

---

[27]John H. French, ed. Gazetteer of the State of New York (Syracuse: R. Pearsall Smith, 1860), p. 429.

[28]James Grant Wilson, ed. The Memorial History of the City of New York (New York: New York History Company, 1893), vol. 3, p. 609.

[29]French, op. cit., p. 429.

# Bibliography

## Primary Sources

Finegan, Thomas E. <u>Free Schools: A documentary History of the Free School Movement in New York State</u>. Albany: University of the State of New York, 1921. 412 pp.
> It is actually more a compilation than a history. The work contains an exhaustive list of primary materials and reprinted sources.

Monroe, Paul. <u>Founding of the American Public School System</u>, <u>Vol. 2</u>. Ann Arbor, Michigan: University Microfilms, 1940. 1775 pp.
> Only volume two is considered a primary source since it is a compilation of all primary sources. These sources document the footnotes of volume one.

Muller, Jr, Alexis. "History of the Public Schools," <u>One Hundred Years of Education</u>. Lockport: Board of Education, 1947. 184pp.
> This work contains official records of the Lockport School System.

<u>New York State Statutes and Laws</u>. (1847). "An Act authorizing the Board of Education of the City and County of New York to establish a Free Academy in said City." Albany: C.Van Benthuysen, pp.208-212.

<u>New York State Statutes and Laws</u>. (1847). "An Act in Relation to Common Schools in the Village of Lockport." Albany: C. Van Benthuysen. pp. 50-62.

<u>New York State Statutes and Laws</u>. (1847). "An Act Establishing Free Schools Throughout the State." Troy: A.W. Scribner and A. West. pp. 192-194.

Randall, Samuel S. <u>History of the Common School System of New York</u>. New York: Ivison, Blakeman, Taylor Company, 1871. 477 pp.
> This work not only contains extracts of speeches and reports given by members of the State Education Board, but of Randall himself.

## Secondary Sources

Bradbury, Anna R. <u>History of the City of Hudson, New York</u>. Hudson: Record Printing
  and Publishing Company, 1908. 233 pp.

Brown, Elmer E. <u>The Making of Our Middle Schools</u>. New York: Longmans, Green and
  Company, 2nd ed., 1926. 547 pp.
     Brown deals with high school development in the United States.

Bruce, Dwight H., ed. <u>Memorial History of Syracuse, New York</u>. Syracuse: H.P.Smith
  and Company, 1891. 849 pp.

Butts, R. Freeman and Lawrence A. Cremin. <u>A History of Education In American
  Culture</u>. 2nd ed. New York: Henry Holt and Company, 1955. 628 pp.

Chace, Franklin H. <u>Syracuse and Its Environs: A History</u>. 3 vols. New York: Historical
  Publishing Company, 1824.

Clarke, T. Wood <u>Utica: A Century and A Half</u>. Utica: The Witman Press, 1952,
  332 pp.

Cooke, Thomas L. <u>Palymyra and Vicinity</u>. Palmyra: Press of the Palmyra Courier
  Journal, 1930. 310 pp.

French, John H. ed. <u>Gazetteer of the State of New York</u>. Syracuse: R. Pearsall Smith,
  1860, 751 pp.

Gifford, Walter J. <u>Historical Development of the New York State High School System</u>.
  Albany: J.B. Lyon Company, 1922. 203 pp.

Hayner, Rutherford. <u>Troy and Rensselear County, New York: A History</u>. 3 vols. New
  York: Lewis Historical Publishing Company, 1925.

Howell, George and Jonathan Tenney, ed. <u>History of the County of Albany from
  1609 to 1886</u>. New York: Munsell and Company, 1886. 997 pp.

Kupka, August. <u>History of Flushing, New York, During the Nineteenth Century</u>.
  Flushing: Flushing Historical Society, 1949. 5 pp.

Larned, J.N. <u>History of Buffalo</u>. 2 vols. New York: Progress of the Empire State
  Company, 1911.

Malone, Dumas. "Samuel Sidwell Randall." <u>Dictionary of American Biography</u>. 20
 vols. New York: C. Scribner's Sons, 1928-1936.

Monroe, Joel H. <u>A Century and a Quarter of History of Geneva</u>. Geneva: W.F.
 Humphrey, Printer and Binder, 1921. 234 pp.

Monroe, Paul. <u>Founding of the American Public School System</u>. 1 vol. New York: The
 MacMillan Company, 1940. 520 pp.

Muller, Alexis, Jr., Lockport, New York, to Jack Block. February 1, 1959. L.S. 1.p.

New Century Club. <u>Outline History of Utica and Vicinity</u>. Utica: L.C. Childs and Sons,
 1900. 210 pp.

Palmer, A. Emerson. <u>The New York Public School</u>. New York: The MacMillan
 Company, 1905. 440 pp.

Platt, Edmund. <u>The Eagle's History of Poughkeepsie</u>: Poughkeepsie: <u>1683 to 1905</u>
 Platt and Platt, 1905. 328 pp.

Randall, Samuel S. <u>History of the State of New York</u>. New York: J.B. Ford and Company, 1871.
 367 pp.
Randall, Samuel S. <u>Common School System of the State of New York</u>. Troy: Johnson
 and Davis, 1851. 408 pp.

Salem's Sons and Daughters. <u>The Salem Book: Records of the Past</u>. Salem: The  Salem
 Review Press, 1896. 250 pp.

Wilson, James, ed. <u>The Memorial History of the City of New York</u>. 4 vols. New York:
 New York History Company, 1893.

# CHAPTER XVI

## GEOGRAPHY

In the days before the telescopic camera or even before the advent of the photograph, all of what one wished to call one's land or property and all of what a nation called its boundaries had to be put in writing. A deed to the land had to be constructed in language form. "One should walk so many paces to the left, proceed to a brook, then turn right to the large oak tree, and walk straight to the hedge…." These and many other words became the basis of land grants as well as verbal arguments, fistfights, and even wars. After these disagreements were peaceably or otherwise settled, maps were drawn, hopefully, from eyewitness accounts or official records.

The maps you see in history texts may or may not be accurate, up-to-date, or useful. Very few have been drawn by eyewitnesses. They may not have been drawn according to the specific directions stated in the original deeds nor land grants. As you know, deeds to property change hands. Property may be added to or broken up. Sections of your town that were once politically independent may have combined to form one large borough or city. What has happened to that particular brook mentioned above? Has it changed its course? Has it dried up and disappeared? And the large oak tree! Is it still there or has it been cut down? And what about that hedge? Has it expanded over time so that the original spot has become indistinguishable from the rest of the stones or bushes? A pace or a single step: Does it still cover as many feet as it once did, or have we grown taller than our ancestors?

Today, in the United States, the deed measures land in feet and inches. But there are still the common boundaries of a small stream, stone hedge, or property that zigzags. Your family's deed may have become the source of some arguments with your neighbors. Upon examining your deed, you discover that those few feet belong to your family. Perhaps, you and your neighbors are sharing land that legally belongs to your town government. You could imagine the embarrassment your family may suffer because of a misunderstanding over the geography of your property.

Let us examine some historical and geographic labels which are frequent causes of ill will. When we say some of our people live in the South, the North, the Southwest, the Northeast, or the Deep South, we should make clear exactly what we mean. For a Southerner to refer to New York City or its suburbs as the East is to ignore the many other areas that are Eastern. However, the individual referring to New York may be thinking of other than geographic limits. Perhaps, that person is considering the New York Stock Exchange as the heart and center of the Eastern financial world. One may be referring to a particular habit or manner of speaking which is common in the New York area. Suddenly, every person who lives in the East has become a New Yorker.

The same reasoning holds true when we speak of the Cotton South, of southern speech, or merely of the South. Isn't it conceivable that not every region in the South grows nor has ever grown cotton? Not all southerners speak alike. The origin, place of residence, level of family income, and social position have a great deal to do with one's dialect, wherever one lives: North,

East, South, or West. There are towns in New Jersey, New York, Pennsylvania, and even regions north of New York State which are more southern in outlook than towns in what is considered the South. We tend to put labels on people and places and let them stay. But, we forget the most important aspect of life and, therefore, of history: change.

The nation has changed even though our traditional image of what once was Southern or Western or Northern may have remained with us. Ask yourself if you are willing to accept change. Does the West still seem to you to be the home of lawless cowboys or the frontier of American civilization? Nevertheless, you are living during a period of great change. People are finding employment in cities, the names of which their parents never heard. They are changing the image of those areas. You are living during a period when people commute by plane or train to New York, Washington, D.C., Atlanta, Chicago and elsewhere from all parts of the country. As the age of supersonic jets continues, you will see so much change that geographic terms which are used now will no longer have meaning in the future.

This change is happening not only in our country, but around the globe. What we once considered as Western nations or non-Western nations have been changing so rapidly that the words "Western" and "non-Western" will soon lose their significance. Boundaries once formed for political reasons are changing because of religious, cultural, or economic ties. Countries that were once enemies are coming together to form permanent unions. The historian of today and of the future must recognize that many official records may contain misleading information, especially if those who are responsible for writing the documents are not careful to make note of changes that occur in international agreements.

Very serious problems in geographic research and analysis still remain with us here on this planet. How may we encourage nations to have respect for each other when they are constantly violating each other's land, waters, air lanes, or even undersea space? Eyewitnesses from the accusing nation may testify to some intrusions. Eyewitnesses from the aggressor nation may offer conflicting testimony. Disputes of this nature are very difficult to solve in an international court. Could the supposed judge and jury have partiality for one or another nation? Of course. National representatives, as human beings, may be biased or prejudiced. They may see things not as they are in reality, but as they want them to be. The tragic result is that the whole world may suffer because of these disputes.

Your era may someday be called the "Age of Outer Space." Who knows what historical, geographic problems will occur when those nations which desire to occupy outer space planets begin to survey the land? Perhaps, the same difficulties which we have experienced on this planet, the same arguments which your own family might have had at one time with your neighbors, will occur among nations over the territories of outer space. Perhaps, your generation will find a way to solve the disputes. Your generation may find some logical means of avoiding wars and other violent encounters over outer space. Let us, also, affirm that yours will be the generation which will solve present problems concerning disputed air and sea lanes, as well as undersea land areas of this world. If you will accomplish these tasks, you will be doing what previous generations could not nor would not do here on earth.

# FOR FURTHER STUDY

Who were our allies in World War I? Our enemies? Who were our allies in World War II? Our enemies? What was the special case of Italy?

To what international alliances or treaty organizations does our country belong today?

Three grants were given by the British government, two in 1606 and one in 1620. Because of the wording in these grants, land disputes developed between the colonies of Virginia and Massachusetts. The grant given to the London Company in 1606 is in the following language:

> … and they shall and may begin their said first Plantation and Habitation at any Place upon the said Coast of Virginia or America, where they shall think fit and convenient, between the said four and thirty, and one and forty Degrees of said Latitude; and that they shall have all Lands…from the said first Seat of their Plantation and Habitation by the Space of fifty Miles of English Statute Measure, all along the said Coast of Virginia and America, towards the West and Southwest, as the Coast lyeth…and also all the lands…from the said Place of their first Plantation and Habitation for the Space of fifty like English Miles, all along the said Coast of Virginia and America, towards the East and Northeast or towards the North, as the Coast Lyeth… and also all the Lands… from the same fifty Miles every way on the Sea Coast, directly into the main Land by the space of one hundred like English Miles. -- William Stith, <u>History of First Discovery</u> <u>and Settlement of Virginia</u>, New York, 1865, Appendix p.2.

The grant given to Plymouth Company in 1606 is in the following words:

> ...they shall and may begin their said Plantation and Seat of their first Abode and Habitation at any Place upon the said Coast of Virginia and America, where they shall think fit and convenient, between eight and thirty Degrees of the said Latitude and five and forty Degrees of the same Latitude; and that they shall have all the Lands...from the first Seat of their Plantation and Habitation by the Space of fifty like English Miles, as is aforesaid, all alongst the said Coast of Virginia and America towards the West and Southwest or towards the South, as the Coast lyeth...and also all the Lands from the said Place of their first Plantation and Habitation for the Space of fifty like Miles all alongst the said coast of Virginia and America towards the East and Northeast or towards the North, as the Coast lyeth...and also all the Lands...from

the same fifty Miles every way on the Sea Coast, directly into the main Land, by the Space of one hundred like English Miles, -- W.Stith, <u>History of First Discovery and Settlement of Virginia</u>, New York, 1865, Appendix, pp. 2-3.


The grant given to the reorganized Plymouth Company known in 1620 as Council for New England is as follows:

> ...all that Circuit, Continent, Precincts, and Limits in America, lying and being in Breadth from Forty Degrees of Northerly Latitude from Equinoctial Line, to Forty-eight Degrees of the said Northerly Latitude, and in Length by all the Breadth aforesaid throughout the Maine Land, from Sea to Sea...called by the Name of New England, in America.--Ebenzer Hazard, <u>Historical Collections Consisting of State Papers and Other Authentic Documents</u>, Philadelphia, 1792-1794, Vol. I, p. 105.


The evidence reproduced above is taken from: <u>Atlas of American History</u>, by James Truslow Adams, p.31, Plate #11, Charles Scribner's Sons, copyright 1943. In addition, the following map showing overlapping boundaries resulting from the wording of the three grants appears in the same text.

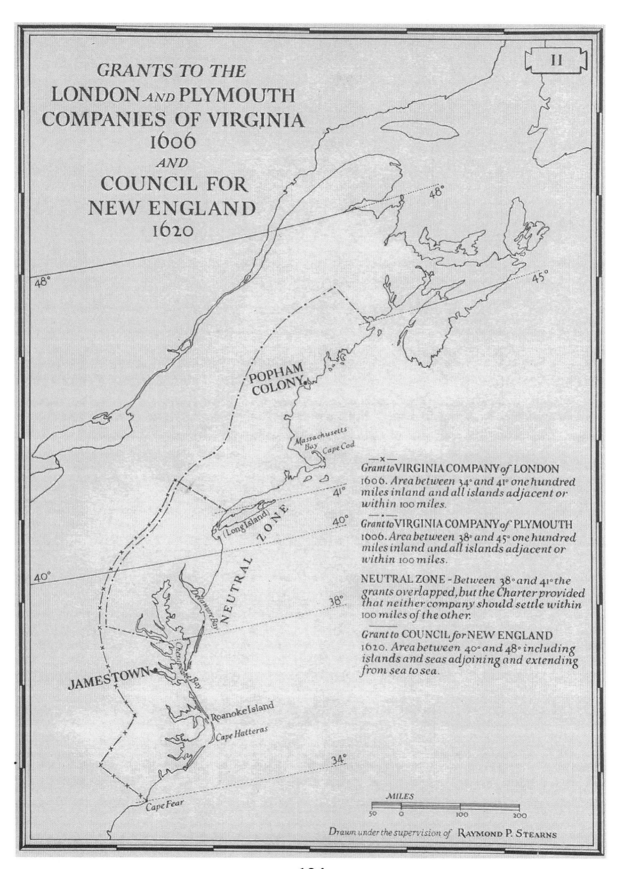

GRANTS TO THE
LONDON AND PLYMOUTH
COMPANIES OF VIRGINIA
1606
AND
COUNCIL FOR
NEW ENGLAND
1620

II

48°

45°

48°

POPHAM
COLONY

Massachusetts
Bay
Cape Cod

41°

40°

(Long Island)

NEUTRAL ZONE

40°

Delaware Bay

38°

JAMESTOWN

Chesapeake Bay

Roanoke Island
Cape Hatteras

34°

Cape Fear

—x— Grant to VIRGINIA COMPANY of LONDON
1606. Area between 34° and 41° one hundred
miles inland and all islands adjacent or
within 100 miles.

Grant to VIRGINIA COMPANY of PLYMOUTH
1606. Area between 38° and 45° one hundred
miles inland and all islands adjacent or
within 100 miles.

NEUTRAL ZONE – Between 38° and 41° the
grants overlapped, but the Charter provided
that neither company should settle within
100 miles of the other.

Grant to COUNCIL for NEW ENGLAND
1620. Area between 40° and 48° including
islands and seas adjoining and extending
from sea to sea.

MILES
50   0        100        200

Drawn under the supervision of RAYMOND P. STEARNS

124

# CHAPTER XVII

## CHARACTER STUDY

This aspect of historical writing is, perhaps, the most difficult of all. Yet, it has most appeal among writers and the reading public. Great skill is required in creating a character study of someone in any historical age. Suppose you were to try to build a character study of one of your friends. You could, but, you would have to work at it. Using your knowledge of the processes of history, you have to consider primary and secondary evidence, evaluate your material externally and internally, and come to conclusions. Finally, you have to develop a synthesis of your friend's character or personality traits.

Remember that not only are you the writer but also a close friend, a primary source. So you have to look at this person objectively, or as we say, "from a distance." How strong a person are you? This may be an excellent way of testing your ability to keep personal bias or favoritism from your work. You must be willing to allow what others say and think of your friend to be heard. If their statements are false, then historical criticism will reveal falsehood. Perhaps, you do not see your friend as he or she appears to others. Are you ready and willing to discredit your own comments as biased or one-sided? All historians who write about national or international figures whom they know have the same problem.

If you have thought about the problem of character analysis, you may find that it is easier to write about someone whom you do not know. This is what a historian must do, especially if the historian is interested in writing about someone who lived long ago. Whether a scholar studies a person who lived centuries ago or is still living, it is best to begin by generalizing in the form of questions. What kind of person was or is...? If the expression, "kind of person," is too vague, the writer may wish to select particular character traits and then phrase each in the form of a question: honesty, sincerity, honor, loyalty, cowardice, generosity, jealousy, and sense of humor. For example, one may ask: "Did George Washington have a sense of humor?"

How often do you discover a trait by accident? One eyewitness account describes a person you are studying as a villain or a coward. Now, you have a lead. But you must do your best in examining that source critically for external authenticity and internal feelings and attitudes. What do you know about the person who wrote such an opinion? Was he or she jealous? A liar? Was the person just joking? Do you realize that you are examining not only the character of the person whom you are studying, but also the character of people who make remarks about others?

Whenever you examine primary and secondary sources which were written many years ago, you may find semantic problems with language. "Semantic" means: having to do with change in the meaning of words through time and usage. To illustrate, examine the word "humor" in the question, "Did George Washington have a sense of humor?" We all know what we mean by this word. However, during the period of American Colonial history, "humor" meant one of the four essential fluids which entered a person's body. The relative proportions of these fluids were believed to determine each person's mental and physical health. So, if you found an account which referred to the humor of George Washington, and that account was written by someone who knew him, perhaps, it referred to Washington's physical illness prior to his death.

In the same way, the word, "flower," which was mentioned in the chapter on chronology, has changed its meaning. Not only in the English language have thousands of words changed their meaning through time, but there have been changes in all other languages. If a writer is studying primary and secondary sources in a foreign language, he or she should become familiar with the semantic problems of that language. Then very old primary or secondary sources may make sense. Otherwise, one may need the help of a linguist.

Do you wonder how an author of a biographical account or historical novel knows what a particular person is like? In other words, how has the character study been composed? Whenever you view a movie based on the life of some historical figure, don't you wonder how so much of the person's private life is convincingly told? You should consider the research, historical investigation, and synthesis required before the filming takes place. What a writer, novelist, or movie producer may want is a well-rounded portrait of the individual in question.

It may seem difficult to secure, but in the long run it makes for more cohesiveness to study a person's character at one stage or time in life. At the age of fifteen, twenty-one, thirty-five, or fifty, what is that person like? A person changes both physically and emotionally at different stages in life. If a historian works from sources which cover a person's complete life record, there may be uncertainty for some conclusions because of differing accounts and opinions. One account written during the early years of the person's life may describe that person as careless, unconcerned, or reckless. However, another account written during the subject's middle-aged life describes the same person as somber, industrious, and careful. It makes no sense to combine these traits because of changes in character and personality.

By building a well-rounded character study of an individual, you may include features of the person's physical and emotional makeup at the same time. For example, if there are any photographs or drawings of the individual taken at a particular stage of life, they will become very useful when you examine the health of the person at a specific time. One's state of health, intelligence, socioeconomic and political views, as well as moral convictions are all important. The individual's hobbies, leisure and sports interests, as well as work habits should not be neglected provided primary or secondary sources are available on these aspects of his or her life. Whatever bits of information you may pick up must be examined for external authenticity and internal psychology.

As you well know, the influence that the family and the community have on the development of an individual's character is worthy of attention and should not be neglected. How does that individual relate to family, relatives, peers, and fellow workers? Examine sources concerning the friends whom President Harding had during his term in the presidency to discover some reasons for Mr. Harding's failure in office. Those friends may have been responsible for literally destroying the president. He died suddenly in 1923. Yet, who knows how much he had suffered emotionally before 1923?

Some mention must be made of hero worship before the close of this chapter. The roots of hero worship originate in several different ways. They may develop as a result of a synthesis done about a leader which exaggerates the good in his or her character. They may stem from conclusions that were inappropriately or carelessly made. After all, from fact or certainty to uncertainty is a very wide range, and it requires patience on the part of the writer to arrive painstakingly at a separate conclusion for each character trait. Perhaps, the general public will not accept nor even allow the reality of a person's character to be revealed. It may call for overt or subtle censorship of sources, especially if people have a high regard for that person. It may be, as was mentioned in the chapter on conclusions, that writers have continued and expanded the theme first developed by an admirer. Whatever the reasons, we have a responsibility when we become writers of history or biographers. We must maintain objectivity. Unless we strive for objectivity, we may become victims of our own propaganda. That is, we shall continue to pass on to society character portraits that worship the individual and protect him or her from any public attack, or we shall continue to degrade the individual and his or her background in order to protect our own image and our own society from any negative criticisms. If we succeed in developing character studies that are objectively presented, we shall have reached the highest goal to which any people may aspire.

# FOR FURTHER STUDY

How do you think the tales of George Washington's boyhood honesty originated? Have you ever heard of the name, Parson Weems?

Read Frederick L. Allen's profile of Warren Harding in <u>Only Yesterday</u>. How does it differ from the version in your history text?

On pages 145 and 146 of the work, <u>The Fall of the Dynasties:  The Collapse of the Old Order 1905-1922</u>, by Edmond Taylor, published by Doubleday and Company in 1963, appears the following information:

> Wilhelm resented his parents, especially his mother, who reserved her pallid affection for her other healthier children; her rejection of him undoubtedly helped to mold the ambivalent feelings toward England that he later manifested.

Wilhelm's father was Prince Friedrich of Prussia; his mother was Queen Victoria's daughter.  Did Wilhelm II, Emperor of Germany during World War I, come to hate his mother's country because of her rejection of him?  What do you think?

Examine the following reproductions.  Notice that the three artists give three different impressions of George Washington.

Painting of George Washington by Charles Willson Peale, 1776.  34.1178

Photo courtesy of The Brooklyn Museum, Dick S. Ramsay Fund.

Painting of George Washington by Rembrandt Peale, 1778-1860.

The Metropolitan Museum of Art, bequest of Frances Mead, 1926 (54.15.1) Image at The Metropolitan Museum of Art.

Painting of George Washington by Adolph Ulrich Wertmuller 1751-1811.

The Metropolitan Museum of Art, bequest of Charles Allen Munn, 1924 (24.109.82)
Image at The Metropolitan Museum of Art.

**Andrew Carnegie, 1850**

**Jack Block**
**The Study of History**
**Dr. Hunt**
**Columbia University**

# PREFACE

This paper has three parts. Part one places the Carnegie family in the year of 1850.

Part two examines Andrew Carnegie and his life during this year. Here, concentration is on the relationship to his parents and to his success as a messenger boy. Interestingly, 1850 is the first financially successful year in the boy's life.

The third and final part deals with a physical description of Andrew Carnegie in 1850 and 1851.

This writer has studied primary and secondary sources for the year of 1850. Although understanding that sources from a later period may help, he believes that certain generalizations may be made mainly using evidence from that year.

# I

In the year 1850, the Carnegie family, which consisted of William, age 44, his wife Margaret, age 34, and their children, Andrew, 14, and Thomas, 6,[1] lived in Alleghany City, Pennsylvania.[2] They rented the rear apartment of a small, black frame house on Rebecca Street, and paid rent to Mrs. Carnegie's relatives.[3]

To add to the already run down condition of the neighborhood, the Alleghany River would now and then rise and overflow onto the homes nearest the waterfront. Because of this, the whole neighborhood looked rather shabby.[4]

Yet, this poor environment did not stop the ambitious young Carnegie from achieving his goals. He set out to better his life and became one of the wealthiest men in the world.

# II

Andrew Carnegie passed his fourteenth birthday in November of 1849.[5] Sometime between November 1849 and April 1850, a transformation took place that was to alter the course of his future life and fortune. Early in 1850, Andrew left a job that offered him no future nor security and took employment in the Pittsburgh office of the Western Union Telegraph Company. He obtained a position as messenger.[6]

Until he started to work for the Pittsburgh branch office of Western Union, Andrew labored as a combination clerk and spool dyer for Mr. John Hay, a manufacturer of bobbins.[7] He received a salary of either $1.65 per week[8] or $2.00 per week.[9] The boy hated the smell of the oil vats in which he had to bathe the spools of cotton. Carnegie later stated in his autobiography, "I never succeeded in overcoming the nausea produced by the smell of oil."[10] He longed to be rid of that phase of his work.

Andrew did enjoy, however, the clerking part of his job. He may have had superior ability and could catch on quickly. Even when he had attended the Rolland School under Mr. Robert Martin in Dunfermline, Scotland, it was said that he was an "apt pupil."[11] According to

---

[1]Andrew Carneigie, Autobiography of Andrew Carnegie, (Boston: Houghton Mifflin Company, 1920), p. 25.
[2] Ibid., p. 30.
[3]James Howard Bridge, The Inside Story of the Carnegie Steel Company (New York: The Aldine Book Company, 1903), p. 13.
[4]Loc.cit.
[5]Andrew Carnegie, op cit., p. 25.
[6]Ibid., p. 36.
[7]Ibid., p.34
[8]Burton J. Hendrick, The Life of Andrew Carnegie (Garden City, New York: Doubleday, Doran and Company, Inc., 1932), vol. 1, p. 52.
[9]Andrew Carnegie, op.cit., p. 34.
[10]Ibid., pp. 35-36.
[11]James B. Mackie, Andrew Carnegie: His Dunfermline Ties and Benefactors (Dunfermline, Scotland: Dunfermline Journal Printing Works, 1916), pp. 39-40.

Mr. Mackie, Mr. Martin spoke of Andrew Carnegie as one of the "smartest lads who ever passed through his school."[12]

The lad kept the books for Mr. Hay.[13] He used the single entry accounting system. During the winter of 1849, Andrew heard that larger firms were beginning to use the double entry accounting system, and he decided to attend a night class in bookkeeping given by a Mr. Williams in Pittsburgh.[14]

For this writer, the question remains: How did Andrew Carnegie obtain this new position of messenger? This opportunity led him to a wealth never before realized by him nor his family. It paid $3.00 a week and offered the child laborer many advantages in the expanding telegraph industry.[15] Furthermore, common and dirty factory work was obviously more tiresome and much less desirable.

In his autobiography, Carnegie writes that one night, when he returned home from work at Mr. Hay's, his Uncle Hogen told him that he knew of a position which was open for Andrew. Mr. David Brooks, manager of the telegraph office in Pittsburg, had asked Uncle Hogen if he knew where "a good boy could be found to act as messenger."[16] Mr. Brooks and Uncle Hogen were checker players and it was during the evening's game that the inquiry was made.[17]

Carnegie further relates that his mother was in favor of having Andrew secure this new position. But his father disapproved because "I was too young and too small...it was evident that a much larger boy was expected."[18] The final family decision was to allow Andrew to "...go over the river to Pittsburgh and call on Mr. Brooks."[19] Father and son went to the office door and Carnegie asked his father to stay outside. Andrew recalls that he wanted to be alone with "...the great man and learn my fate." He also stated that he could "...make a smarter showing if alone with Mr. Brooks than if my good old Scotch father were present, perhaps to smile at my airs."[20] The result of the interview was that he obtained the job.[21]

A careful analysis of the sources available for the above account shows that the account, although primary and first hand, is not reliable. When one reads the autobiography, one is left with the impression that Andrew Carnegie had to do it all on his own. He wanted no help, even from his family. As a matter of fact, he even offers advice to his readers that they should do everything for themselves. In essence, this is how one becomes a self-made man.[22]

---

[12]Loc.cit.
[13]Andrew Carnegie, op. cit., p. 36.
[14]Loc.cit.
[15]Barnard Alderson, Andrew Carnegie:  The Man and His Work (New York: Doubleday, and Company, 1902), p. 18.
[16]Andrew Carnegie, op. cit., p.36.
[17]Loc.cit.
[18]Andrew Carnegie, op. cit., p. 37.
[19]Ibid., p. 37.
[20]Ibid., pp. 37-38.
[21]Ibid., p.39.
[22]Loc.cit.

Mr. Burton J. Hendrick, who wrote the longest biography of Carnegie that is available, takes what Carnegie said about obtaining his new job at face value.[23]  Yet, it is surprising that Mr. Hendrick, having included more primary sources in his study then any other biographer of Carnegie, ignored the findings of other biographers of an earlier period.  Take, for example, the work of Mr. J.B. Mackie.[24]  Mr. Mackie, in his study of Carnegie, refers to an account written some time before Carnegie's autobiography was published.  Carnegie wrote the following;

> After filling this position [for Mr. Hay] for some time I heard that boys were wanted in the Ohio Telegraph Office in Pittsburgh.  I felt as though my fortune would be made if I could get into that office, so my father went with me and persuaded the superintendent, James R Reid, to employ me.  Mr. Reid often told me, in later years, that he remembered exactly how I looked that morning in my little blue jacket, with my white hair.[25]

It is clear that there is a discrepancy in the available evidence.  The reliability is lowered by the fact that Carnegie gives two different versions of his childhood experience.  In the Mackie reference, the father has played a dominant role.  It is he who has obtained the job of messenger for his son.  In the autobiography, however, the father is given an inferior status.  He seems to be more of a hindrance than a help to his son.  Which of these versions is then the true account?

This writer has examined the works of two other biographers, Mr. Barnard Alderson and Mr. Herbert Casson, who agree that Andrew's father actually helped him obtain the job as messenger.  Mr. Alderson reveals that Carnegie senior and Mr. Reid were from the same town of Dunfermline, and when Mr. Reid became aware of this, he promised the father that he would employ Andrew.[26]  Mr. Casson states essentially the same in his biography.[27]  It must be pointed out, however, that neither one of these writers documents his statements concerning the account.  Mr. James Reid, in 1879,[28] wrote a history of the telegraph company and mentioned its founders, promoters, and noted men.  In his account, he briefly mentions that in 1850 a lad from his own native land, Andrew Carnegie, was employed in the Pittsburgh branch.[29]

There is a problem because all biographers mentioned rely on statements of Andrew Carnegie.  Since he himself has two conflicting versions, no conclusions can be drawn as to certainty, probability or possibility on either side.

In referring to his relationship with his father, Andrew Carnegie writes that his parent was "…one of nature's noblemen, beloved by all, a saint."[30]  Yet, Andrew, according to the sources available, did not take after his father.  The elder Carnegie lacked the spirit, drive, and

---

[23]Burton, J. Hendrick, op.cit., pp. 55-57.
[24]James B. Mackie, op.cit., p. 72.
[25]Loc.cit.
[26]Barnard Alderson, op. cit., p. 17.
[27]Herbert N. Casson, The Romance of Steel (New York:  A.S. Barnes and Company, 1907). p. 70.
[28]James D. Reid, The Telegraph in America:  Its Founders, Promoters, and Noted Men (New York: Derby Brothers, 1879) p.177.
[29]Loc.cit.
[30]Andrew Carnegie, op.cit., p. 33.

energy his son possessed.[31]  Andrew may have respected and loved him, but the son could not really count on his father for financial support.[32]  The father was never able to recover from the effects of displacement of the home cottage industry.  In 1848, he left Scotland with his family and hoped to continue his trade as a weaver[33] in Alleghany city, where his wife's relatives lived.[34]  He found no opportunity and had to accept work in a bobbin factory as a common laborer.[35]  Andrew soon entered the same factory as a bobbin boy and outlasted his father on the job.[36]  Whereas, Andrew waited until he found another job (with a Mr. Hay) before he left the factory, William quit and went back to his old habit of weaving tablecloths and occasionally peddled them door to door.[37]  The available sources do not suggest that he ever went back to work on a permanent basis.

What was Andrew's attitude toward his mother?  This writer paid little attention to Elbert Hubbard's remark that "Andrew Carnegie is the son of his mother,"[38] until he examined the existing evidence.  During Andrew's early life in Allegheny City and while he worked as messenger in 1850, Andrew's mother was ambitiously employed.  Carnegie stated that when his father could not work at the factory, his mother came to the rescue.[39]  "In her youth she had learned to bind shoes in her father's business for pin money, and the skill then acquired was now turned to account for the family."[40]  She earned four dollars a week by binding shoes during the evening hours and often worked until midnight.[41]  Margaret Carnegie had drive and energy. Andrew may have been inspired by her persistence and her tireless efforts to raise her family's standard of living.  His devotion to her was exceedingly strong.  He often said that he could never adequately estimate all that he owed to her strong will, her far seeing judgment, and her loving, and motherly sympathy.[42]  It was she who possibly encouraged him to climb to the top successfully.[43]

James D. Reid says of Andrew Carnegie in 1850 that he was "…prompt, intelligent and industrious; was happy with his three dollars a week and performed his duties well and cheerfully."[44]  This is the only primary account available regarding his working attitudes.  In another account, Mr. Reid gives testimony as to the boy's ambition.  "He had not been with me a month when I began to instruct him and found him an apt pupil.  He spent all his spare time in

[31]Burton J. Hendrick, op. cit., pp. 51-52.
   Elbert Hubbard, Little Journeys to the Homes of Great Business Men (East Aurora, Roycroft Printers, 1909). p. 34.
   Allen Johnson, "Andrew Carnegie," Dictionary of American Biography (New York: Charles Scribiner's Sons, 1928-1936), vol.3, p. 499.
   Barnard Alderson, op.cit., pp. 6-7.
[32]Burton J. Hendrick, op.cit., pp. 51-52.
   Andrew Carnegie, op.cit., p. 31.
[33]James Burnley, Millionaires and Kings of Enterprise (London: Harmsworth Brothers, Ltd., 1901). p. 3.
[34]Andrew Carnegie, op.cit., p. 3.
[35]Ibid., p. 34.
[36]Burton J. Hendrick, op.cit., pp. 51-52.
[37]Loc.cit.
[38]Elbert Hubbard, op .cit., p. 34.
[39]Andrew Carnegie, op. cit., p. 31.
[40]Loc.cit.
[41]Loc.cit.
[42]Barnard Alderson, op. cit., pp. 6-7.
[43]Ibid., p.7.
[44]James D. Reid, op. cit., p. 177.

practice…. Soon he could do as well as I could at the keys….”[45] Carnegie tells his readers that he was ambitious. By his own account, he was so anxious to become a good messenger quickly that "Before long I could shut my eyes and beginning at the foot of a business street call off the names of the firms in proper order.”[46] Because there is no conflicting evidence, primary nor secondary, it is certain that Andrew Carnegie was an ambitious youngster.

Mr. Bridge wrote that Andrew, who was older than most of the boys, had a kind of assertiveness which other messengers regarded as evidence of “… fitness for leadership.”[47] According to Mr. Harlow, it was not long before Andrew began to assume leadership and responsibility for handing out the messages and assigning them to other messengers for delivery.[48] It may be assumed that these boys, the majority of whom were Rebecca Street neighbors, were a bit jealous of him. It was through Andrew's control that they had a steady job,[49] and since Andrew received the messages before they did, he could pick out the ones that were more lucrative for his own delivery. Andrew states that these boys who were his close friends often quarreled as to who should take the special messages which brought a 10 cent tip. Carnegie proposed that the boys pool the tips at the end of each week and divide the money equally. They agreed and appointed Andrew as treasurer, "Peace and good humor reigned ever afterwards.”[50]

But Mr. Winkler offers a completely different account:

> Andy, it must be confessed, was not very popular with the other boys in the Telegraph office. The youngsters got an extra dime for delivering messages beyond a certain limit. Andy was greedy for these assignments. Finally the extra money was pooled and divided evenly at the end of the week.[51]

However, we may not overlook what Carnegie says about his working relationships. No other first-hand account is available.

Only Mr. Hendrick and Mr. Winkler include any evidence of early writings of Andrew Carnegie. Mr. Hendrick quotes a letter written in 1852 by the boy to his uncle in Scotland. In the letter, Andrew stands against the institution of slavery and favors the political party opposed to slavery, the Free Soil Democrats.[52]

This view of slavery is in keeping with the aggressive and ambitious qualities of Carnegie's personality. He actually favors a party which believes strongly in free competition. He stands with and for the self-reliant, self-made individual who resents any interference with his right to work on a free and competitive basis.

---

[45]James Burnley, op. cit., p. 5.
[46]Andrew Carnegie, op. cit., p. 39
[47]James Howard Bridge, op. cit., p. 15.
[48]Alvin F. Harlow, Andrew Carnegie, (New York: Julian Messner, Inc., 1953). p. 28.
[49]Ibid. p. 26.
[50]Andrew Carnegie, op. cit., p. 43.
[51]John K. Winkler, The Life of Andrew Carnegie (1835-1919). (New York: The Vanguard Press, 1931). p. 48.
[52]Burton J. Hendrick, op. cit., p. 48.

This interpretation may be more clearly seen when one looks at his social and economic views. In the excerpt quoted by Mr. Winkler, Carnegie, at 15, writes an essay on Labor.[53] In essence, he says that labor is necessary for all to survive. Nature does not provide a substitute for labor. "It is high time that drones should occupy at least the lowest position in society. A working man is a more useful citizen and ought to be more respected than an idle prince."[54]

These few lines and the previous letter may be of more value than his views in his autobiography. Here are his thoughts about himself while he is still young and seeking recognition. He is seeking status in a growing, competitive, and industrial nation. In his mind, recognition and status will come to the ambitious and clever individual.

With this knowledge, one may realize why Carnegie writes years later in his autobiography how important it is for the youth of this type to gain recognition. Speaking of his first year as a messenger boy, Carnegie writes, "I do not know of a situation in which a boy is more apt to attract attention, which is all a really clever boy requires in order to rise. Wise men are always looking out for clever boys."[55]

## III

Two primary sources are available which describe Andrew Carnegie's physical characteristics in the year 1850. The first is taken from the autobiography and the second from the statements of James Reid, Andrew's employer at the telegraph company. Andrew himself says that he has white hair and that he is small for his age.[56] When he was interviewed for the job, Carnegie adds that a messenger asked Mr. Brooks, "What on earth are you going to do with such a little fellow as that? He's too small for the job."[57] Mr. Reid corroborates Andrew's testimony. He notices the white hair as soon as he first meets Andrew.[58] Elsewhere, he states, "… in 1850 a little lad named Andrew Carnegie,"[59] and "I liked the boy's looks and it was easy to see, though he was little, he was full of spirit."[60]

No primary or secondary sources state Andrew's exact height. Words like "small" or "small for his age" do not accurately describe him. The best that this writer is able to establish is that Carnegie was shorter than most boys of fourteen years of age. Mr. Hendrick compares Andrew to his father and writes, "In appearance the two were not unlike; both were small for their years; both tow-headed, both blue eyed…."[61] Mr. Harlow adds two other details in his description such as "…when the Carnegies first settled in Alleghany, Andrew, undersized, square jawed, with eyes set wide apart and hair so flaxen that it was almost white…."[62]

---

[53] John K. Winkler, op. cit., p. 51.
[54] Loc.cit.
[55] Andrew Carnegie, op. cit., p. 43.
[56] Ibid., p. 35.
[57] Ibid., p. 39.
[58] James D. Reid, op. cit., p. 177.
[59] James Burnley, op. cit., p. 5.
[60] Loc.cit.
[61] Burton J. Hendrick, op. cit., p. 14.
[62] Alvin F. Harlow, op. cit., p. 15.

Only one photograph of Carnegie at the age of sixteen is available in any work which this writer examined. This picture, selected for the autobiography, appears on page 185.[63] Whether or not it is the best likeness will not be known until other likenesses are made available. Part of the same photograph appears in Mr. Hendrick's biography.[64] Thus, this writer concludes that it is a fact that Andrew Carnegie, at the age of fifteen, had white hair. It is also a fact that he was physically smaller than other boys with whom he worked in 1851.

[63]Andrew Carnegie, op. cit., p. 185.
[64]Burton J. Hendrick, op. cit. p.14.

# Bibliography

## Primary Sources

Carnegie, Andrew,  <u>An Address to the Students of Cornell University, April 26, 1907</u>.  New York: Press of M.J. Roth. 26 pp.
    In this address, Mr. Carnegie discusses  his working experience as a boy and emphasizes the rise of a self-made man.

Carnegie, Andrew,  <u>Autobiography of Andrew Carnegie with Illustration</u>. Boston:  Houghton Mifflin Company, 1920. 385 pp.

Carnegie, Andrew,  "How I Served My Apprenticeship."  <u>The Youth's Companion</u>.  (April 23, 1896), Reprinted in <u>The Gospel of Wealth</u>.  New York:  The Century Company, 1900. Reprinted in <u>Heritage of America</u>.  Rev.ed., Boston:  D.C. Heath and Company, 1949. pp. 947-955.
    Mr. Carnegie recalls his early struggles to earn a living in America.  This information later appears in his autobiography.

Carnegie, Andrew, <u>The Empire of Business</u>.  Garden City:  Doubleday, Page and Company, 1902, Reprinted 1971. 384 pp.
    Here again, Mr. Carnegie presents the theme of a self-made man in the beginning chapters.

Reid, James D.  <u>The Telegraph in America:  Its Founders, Promoters, and Noted Men</u>.  New York:  Derby Brothers, 1879. 846 pp.
    Not only does Mr. Reid discuss Mr. Carnegie in 1850, but he reveals his own ideas and impressions of the telegraph industry.

Wilson, Margaret Barcley, ed.  <u>A Carnegie Anthology</u>.  New York:  Press of the American Lithographic Company, 1915. 265 pp.
    The book contains writings of Andrew Carnegie and photographs taken of him during his life.

## Secondary Sources

Alderson, Barnard, <u>Andrew Carnegie The Man and His Work</u>. New York: Doubleday, Page and Company, 1902. 232 pp.
>  Mr. Alderson brings into this account a good deal of material about Alleghany City in the 1850's, especially the Rebecca Street district.

Bridge, James Howard, <u>The Inside Story of the Carnegie Steel Company</u>. New York: The Aldine Book Company, 1903. 369 pp.
>  Although the book is slanted against Carnegie, Mr. Bridge does not write damagingly about Mr. Carnegie's childhood. He also brings to us details about the Rebecca Street district.

Burnley, James, <u>Millionaires and Kings of Enterprise</u>. London: Harmsworth Brothers, Limited, 1901. 513 pp.
>  When Mr. Burnley refers to Mr. Carnegie's youth he offers material that is not documented, especially the remarks of Mr. James Reid.

Casson, Herbert N, <u>The Romance of Steel</u>. New York: A.S. Barnes and Company, 1907. 373 pp.
>  Mr. Casson gives to his readers the impression that they are there at the scene. Although the style of writing provides an intimate account, the book has no documentation.

Harlow, Alvin M. <u>Andrew Carnegie</u>, New York. Julian Messner, Inc., 1953. 182 pp.
>  This is the latest of the biographies; but it is disappointing because Mr. Harlow tells us nothing new except one piece of information about the boy's appearance. However, he may have used the photograph which appears in Andrew Carnegie's autobiography.

Hendrick, Burton J, <u>The Life of Andrew Carnegie</u>. 2 vols. New York: Doubleday, Doran and Company, 1932.
>  This work, although secondary, contains more primary material than any other secondary work. In the introduction, Mr. Hendrick states that he was given official access to the Carnegie papers by the Carnegie family.

Hubbard, Elbert, <u>Little Journeys to the Homes of Great Business Men: Andrew Carnegie</u>. East Aurora, New York: Roycroft Printers, 1909, 66 pp.
>  Although amusing, the work does not stand the tests of external and internal examination.. As an example, the author states that Mr. Carnegie had red hair.

Johnson, Allen, "Andrew Carnegie," <u>Dictionary of American Biography</u>. 20 vols. New York: Charles Scribner's Sons, 1928-1936.

Mackie, J. B, <u>Andrew Carnegie: His Dunfermline Ties and Benefactors</u>. Dunfermline, Scotland: Dunfermline Journal Printing Works, 1916. 141 pp

Although the work is the only one available by someone who lived in Scotland, it must stand the tests for external and internal criticism.

Winkler, John K, <u>The Life of Andrew Carnegie (1835-1919)</u>. New York: the Vanguard Press, 1931. 307 pp.
   This is the most damaging of all biographies that this writer has studied. It is interesting to examine this work because it gives an entirely different account of Carnegie's life and personality than Carnegie gives of himself.

# CHAPTER XVIII

## BOOK REVIEWING

Tomorrow, when you examine a work of fiction or non-fiction on the subject of history, ask yourself if you are able to read it in the same way you used to. The words, "historical research," "historical method," and "historiography," may have become part of your everyday vocabulary. Hopefully, you have become critical of what you read. Why not review a work as the historian does?

Start with the purpose of the book. Why was it written? Perhaps, the author has found new evidence that may change previously held conclusions. If so, the scholar may wish to present a summary of his or her synthesis in the introduction or final chapter. Even the jacket of the book may reveal a new interpretation. A fresh point of view may be well received by the public. The young generation seems to want new ideas. Young people may want to see the past in a new light.

Examine the scope of the work. A brief survey of the writing will enable you to see in what direction or directions the author is headed. Whenever you examine the scope of a work, you are noticing the breadth, distance covered, or the chronology discussed by the writer. For example, find a study on the American Revolution. Notice how much geographic coverage there is. Is there a section in the book on the European involvement in the war with England? Are there any references to the allies which both the mother country and the colonists had? As for chronological coverage, some authors believe that one must go back to the period of the 1690s to understand fully the origins of the revolution; others date the beginning of the war in the middle 1700s. If you were to write a study of American young people today, how far back in time would you go to discover the origin of the new generation's opinions and behavior? In other words, what would be your chronological scope?

Next, inspect the organization and content of the work. Notice if the author seems to spend too much time on battles. The table of contents may reveal whether the author is ignoring the problems of running the war from the civilian point of view. Does the author take a chronological or topical approach? Chronological approach means that he or she follows the events day-by-day as they happen. However, in a topical approach the author is free to choose those topics which he or she feels will best explain the war. There may be chapters on financing the war, political unity or disunity during the revolution, and social problems within the colonies created by the conflict with the mother country. Now, think of the book you may want to write about your generation. Does it make sense to take a chronological or topical approach? Why? Whichever method you use, you will notice that your approach will govern the organization and content of your work.

We come to the author's style of writing. This is something about which you know a great deal. Like Santa Claus, you know if the author is "bad or good." You know if the writer bores you or if he or she creates interest and excitement. Does the author write too much or too little in a particular chapter? You know if you are able to move through the work easily. Expressions and idioms used should be considered. Would you recommend the work to others? Why? Why not?

From style, turn to illustrations selected for the work. See if reprints of portraits, photographs, maps, charts, and drawings show painstaking research and evaluation or neglect of each. Suppose you come across a particular painting of the Battle of Lexington. You will recall that this battle took place in April, 1775 and is considered to have been the first battle of the American Revolution. The author may have deliberately or unknowingly selected a reprint that portrays the Americans as the winners of the battle. Try to identify why the author has selected that particular illustration. Is the name of the artist mentioned? Was he or she a first- hand observer of the scene painted or sketched? Notice the choice of maps. How useful are they? A good map should be simply designed and vital to the narrative. Cramming of too much detail may destroy its usefulness. The author may even refer to places in the text that have not been indicated on the map. As for charts and diagrams, notice if they have been composed from primary and/or secondary information given in the narrative. Are there allowances made for varying estimates—in other words, what is the range from fact to uncertainty?

If you are writing about your generation, somewhere in the narrative you should explain why you have chosen a particular painting of an individual, a group of individuals, scenes, photographs, maps, charts, and any other visual material. You must explain to your reader why you have made the selection from hundreds and, perhaps, thousands of illustrative materials. As you already know, the selection that you make will reflect your point of view, your attitude toward the society about which you have written. The final choice of visual materials will depend on the synthesis you have formulated.

Should you examine the author's bibliography? Absolutely. The bibliography is a listing of published and/or unpublished sources that the writer has studied and has made some use of in the text. You may find the listing of works used at the end of the book, at the end of each chapter or section. At a glance, you may question details about the bibliography. Are the sources recently published or were they published many years ago? Is there coverage of published and unpublished diaries, journals, memoirs, notes, family papers, governmental and organizational documents, newspapers, or magazine accounts? Has the author taken the trouble to list the primary and secondary sources used in the work? Some writers may include pages of bibliographical references. Others may mention a few references. Remember that you are judging that writer's work, and you must be able to learn the origin of statements and ideas. If you are unable to determine the origin, the error is the historian's not yours.

In examining the bibliography, consider several other factors. Some have already been pointed out. Those that remain are equally important. You should notice references published in foreign countries. Are the titles of these works in their original language or have they been translated into English? When a writer has referred to a foreign source, he or she may want to preserve the accuracy of the language and lessen the chances of errors in translation. The scholar may also wish to demonstrate the extent of curiosity and willingness to hunt for and track down accounts. You may remember that during our revolution, Benjamin Franklin sailed to France to ask for aid from the French government. Scholars are not in agreement as to who actually helped

Franklin. Was it the French Minister, Louis XVI, the king's wife, or all three? A historian with knowledge of the French language and interest in this question could study the sources.

The writer may ask for help from, or as we say, collaborate with a French historian interested in the question of French military aid to the American colonies. Perhaps, in the same way, you may want to know how the young generation in France or in any other country feels about any issues today. You may arrange to collaborate with a foreign writer and publish your work jointly. In that case, both your names will appear on the title page. You are co-authors.

Become curious about the names of publishers and places of publication or printing which appear in the bibliography. Of course, if the writer of the American Revolution has used a work which is very old and rare, the front pages of the reference may have disintegrated. Then, the bibliography may not include this information. However, the author whose book you review should tell you about the loss of vital information. The reasons for knowing the publisher's name and the place of publication and printing are obvious, especially during periods of hostility between nations or among groups of people within one country. The extent to which the scholar is willing to refer to different sides of arguments will reveal objectivity. A writer may have taken out of a country some important documents or other primary sources which may make the work valuable. Sometimes, material is taken out of a geographic area secretly, is printed on a simple printing press for distribution, and is later given to a publisher for legal publication. Who will print the material? It may be a well-known publisher with a record of fairness to all parties concerned, or one who is interested in only material favorable to his or her point of view. Perhaps, the publisher may be some individual without any interest in objectivity, but in propaganda.

Has the author annotated the bibliography? By annotating the bibliography, one writes a few lines about each source used. The annotation helps us to notice which works have been of value to the writer and which have been of minor assistance. In this way, we learn how the historian has used those works. The annotations are short evaluations of sources of information.

It is natural to turn next to the footnotes in the work under review. Notice how the author has made use of those sources listed in the bibliography. There are authors of historical works who do not footnote their information. But this neglect is inexcusable. You want to know exactly where the writer obtained information. The bibliographical annotation does not show the exact page or pages which were used for the particular remark made by our writer. You have a right to know the origin of that remark. The author has an obligation to tell you. Otherwise, if you want to verify the remark in the reference the writer has used, you have to read the entire reference in order to find the exact place where the author obtained information.

What else do footnote citations tell us besides the exact pages used for information? They may tell us how frequently the author, whose book we have been examining, has relied on either primary or secondary sources. If a footnote should refer to a letter written by General George Washington, we may tell at a glance how interested our author is in going back to original sources. Footnotes also tell us how thoroughly the author wants to back up statements. Some chapters may contain many citations, while others may contain a few or none. One may question, with good cause, why there is an absence of citations, especially when the material is based on events with which you, I, and the average reader are not familiar.

Although the bibliography may list many sources, footnote citations tell us at a glance the references which were selected to support the evidence our author has given. The first time a source is cited the complete bibliographic notation is given. The second time the source is mentioned the footnote tells us the name of the author or editor of the reference, the title of the work, and page number from which the author has taken the information. What more do we ask of any writer? Of course, we expect professional honesty. We should expect that when a citation is given, we may, if we choose, go to the exact place in the reference to see for ourselves the original wording.

At this point, we turn our attention to the index of the work. Again, at a glance, we notice how carefully the index was arranged. How considerate is the writer of readers? For example, notice the word "army." If the index has not been carefully prepared, you will find the word, "army," followed by page numbers, such as army: pp. 4; 5; 100; 150; 200. We must now examine each of these pages to discover what is being said about the military. However, in a good index, you will find additional notes: army: financing of, p. 4; moral attitudes toward, p. 5; physical training, p. 100; adjustment to civilian life, p. 150; desertions, p. 200. Whenever you wish to do writing, you should show the same courtesy to your readers as demonstrated in the latter example.

Finally, no discussion of a general review of any historical work is complete without analysis of the scholarship of the author. Do not be surprised if one chapter is better written than others. It may be because of greater effort given to a particular topic. Perhaps, the writer may have a superior background and understanding of a certain aspect of the American Revolution. The author may have a better background in the battles fought in New England than those fought in the South. He or she may know more about social problems created by the conflict with England than about military strategy used by both sides. As you read, identify critical evaluation of sources. Are words such as "external" and "internal" evaluations mentioned in the narrative? How does the writer draw conclusions, based upon what evidence? Does the scholar mention such terms as "fact," "probability," "possibility," and "uncertainty"?

The best way to evaluate the scholarship of an author is to thoroughly examine a selected chapter, but not the first nor last. Most likely, the introductory chapter will set the stage for the narrative and may be a summary of previous events which have led to the main event or topic of the book. Often, the final chapter will combine the central ideas covered in previous chapters. Therefore, nothing new is added. There is no reason to expect the author to footnote material in the concluding chapter. Now, select a chapter for critical review. Follow the evidence to whatever sources it leads you. Examine every given footnote as fully as you are able. When searching for the exact page of a source referred to in the footnote citation, do not become alarmed if what is said on that page has nothing to do with the material in the chapter you are reviewing. You have found an error in external evaluation of the author's writing. If the narrative is externally correct, notice how the author discusses the information acquired from that page reference. In other words, what does internal evaluation reveal? Notice if the author on the

American Revolution has slanted the ideas presented in primary and secondary references in order to stress a point of view

When reviewing a work of historical fiction, you will not have the aid of footnotes nor bibliography to help you in critical evaluation. If you are fortunate, the writer may present in the introduction or in the epilogue some explanation for the synthesis the writer paints with words. You will have to do analysis on your own in order to appraise the historical worth and accuracy of the work. How close to reality does the novel, play, or profile come? Are there any new characterizations of historical figures offered? Has the author attempted to blend into the scene and dialogue any primary source material? Notice how much of the narrative is both externally authentic and internally objective. Try to single out a small section of the work to examine critically.

No matter what kind of historical material you review, fiction or non-fiction, in your mind should run questions such as these: Does the writer discuss earlier or new interpretations (syntheses) of other scholars? Does the author attempt to show why he or she has or has not accepted these previously held syntheses? What is the worth of the writer's contribution to the study of history? It is important that you have the courage to stand up to the most respected writers in the field and ask, "How do you know? What is your proof? Prove it to me." Do not underestimate your ability to do so.

## FURTHER STUDY

When reviewing a work on a historical topic, examine visual material that has been selected.  On the following pages appear two paintings showing Captain John Smith's rescue by Pocahontas.

The paintings were done by two artists during the 1800s.  Each photograph had been retouched by the Library of Congress for possible offense of subject matter to certain people.

What differences do you notice between the two paintings?

Photo courtesy of the Library of Congress.

EVENTS OF INDIAN HISTORY.
Capt. Smith rescued by Pocahontas.

Photo courtesy of Library of Congress

# A Review of <u>The American Revolution</u><br><u>1775 – 1783</u>

**Jack Block**
**The Study of History**
**Dr. Hunt**
**Columbia University**

# PREFACE

This paper has two parts.

Part one is a general review of John Richard Alden's writing on the American Revolution.

Part two is a critical examination of a portion of the work. The chapter chosen for study is entitled, "Long Island to Morristown."

**Part I**

The American Revolution 1775-1783, a work of two hundred ninety-four pages, is part of the New American Nation series published by Harper Brothers Company. The purpose of this series, the second to be published by Harper, is stated by the editors, Professors Morris and Commager. It is their intention to bring about an "authoritative synthesis of the historical scholarship" of today [xiii]. Works like The American Revolution 1775-1783 are said to be based upon new sources and evidence unavailable to the authors of the first series, fifty years prior. [xiii-xiv].

The author, John Richard Alden, who has spent most of his life in the Middle West of the United States, is a trained historian. He has studied at the University of Michigan, where he received a Ph.D. in history and, at present, teaches history at the University of Nebraska.[1] Like other historians, he has had to track down the available sources. It is difficult to estimate how much research Mr. Alden did on his book at the University of Michigan or Nebraska. One may guess that he spent a good portion of his time at such places as the New York Public Library and Historical Society, as well as at other institutions for research along the Eastern seaboard [pp. 93, 140].

Professor Alden has his own purpose in writing the book. Although a revisionist, he states that he has tried to defend the thought and conduct of the patriots in their cause of revolution. At the same time, he is seeking to view the history as objectively as possible [xvii].

When one examines this work one finds that the scope is larger than one may expect from the title. In the first place, Professor Alden goes back to the developments that led to 1775, both in Britain and in the colonies. He actually begins with the year 1763 [pp. 1-5] and works up to the war and its aftermath.

In the second place, the author does not confine himself to a study of the geographic area of the Eastern seaboard in revolutionary America. Instead, he reaches out across the Atlantic to the British Isles, as well as to France and Spain. He even shows the back country of the colonies which is so often neglected in school books.

As for content and organization of his work, Mr. Alden explains that approximately one half is devoted to warfare [xvii]. Yet, he believes that he has gone further than most historians do in similar works into British and European scenes during the era of revolution. Mr. Alden feels that such background will aid in a fuller understanding of this period of American history.

Mr. Alden moves right into the battle of Lexington and follows the major campaigns through New England, Canada, New York, New Jersey, and Pennsylvania. He has both a chronological and topical approach. From chapters two through nine, he follows the campaign in chronological order. However, at this point, he adopts a topical approach and in the next four chapters takes up such matters as economic and political goals of the war as well as secret alliances which the Americans desired with France and Spain. In the final four chapters, the author returns to a chronological study of the close of the Revolutionary War.

---

[1] Who's Who in America "John Richard Alden" (Chicago: Marquis Publications, 1899-1955), vol. 28, p.37.

Mr. Alden's style is interesting apart from his historical interpretations of the period. One cannot say that he is boring to read. He whips up interest and excitement in the battles that occur, and before the reader becomes exhausted with war, he provides a rest. Instead of observing battles, one reads of meetings of diplomats, of plotting for aid from France, and of counter plans of the British and her mercenaries.

At no time are the chapters too long. The longest chapters entitled, "Long Island to Morristown" is twenty-two pages in length [vii]. One moves quickly throughout the book. At all times, Mr. Alden is so clear that the average reader of American history may easily follow him. However, the author does not achieve perfection in presenting his material.

The illustrations used are disappointing. Although Mr. Alden has taken pains to find a portrait of each American and British notable mentioned, he has neglected to analyze each likeness externally and internally. If he were not a historian, Mr. Alden could be forgiven. However, he follows too many rules of historical methodology to have forgotten the importance of analyzing portraits before the age of photography [p. 140].

For examples, take the portrait of George Washington and the scene depicting the Battle of Lexington. Mr. Alden includes a reproduction of a portrait of George Washington painted by James Peale. The author makes no comment as to the reliability of this likeness. Nor does he mention that the Peale portrait is one of several different likenesses of George Washington. To the untrained eye, the portrait is sufficient. But, Mr. Alden writes as a trained historian and must consider the accuracy of any likeness presented in his book. The same lack of critical evaluation is obvious for the remainder of the portraits used.

As for the scene depicting the battle of Lexington, Mr. Alden chooses a print dated 1798, from the New York Historical Society [p.140]. This work has a decidedly aggressive quality in the position of the patriots. The painting by Ralph Earle suggests that the patriots are prepared for the battle, are hidden behind trees, and are defying the British. Yet, no mention is made that there are several other paintings of this battle and that each offers a different version of the Battle of Lexington.

One of the most serious charges against Mr. Alden is that his maps, although praised by a reviewer,[2] are for the most part worthless. In general, they do not adequately explain nor identify what is told in the narrative. This writer, more than once, had to consult additional maps not included in the text in order to locate the position of the British or Colonial forces described in the narrative [pp. 123, 229]. The only sensible maps are on pages 37 and 137. They are simple and follow the narrative completely.

Mr. Alden's bibliography, although exhaustive, does not reach the standard of scholarship it should have. Many of the works cited are not annotated. One is not able to tell if Mr. Alden has read each fully or has included works because they deal with the same topic. The author does, however, take pains to recommend a varied bibliography to the reader.

---

[2]Richard Johnson, San Francisco Chronicle. (Feb 14, 1954) p.27.
Metrice M. James and Dorothy Brown, eds., The Book Review Digest. (1954) p.7. As taken from Richard Johnson, p.27.

There are special sections which list diaries, journals, memoirs, newspapers, biographies, general secondary histories as well as suggested military, economic, social, political, and diplomatic histories of the revolutionary period. Included are various guides to public documents and special collections of the governments of the United States, Britain, France, and Spain [pp.269-283].

How should the index be rated? It is not always useful. In several locations, names given in the index have numerical listings of pages to see, but no other explanations. Take for example, the word, "Loyalists" [p.290]. The author gives thirty different pages on which this word, or reference to it, appears. But in no case does the author explain the reason for the numerical listing.

How is one to judge Mr. Alden's entire work? Since Mr. Alden is a historian, he must be judged on the same basis that this writer would judge any historian. How well does he use the historical method? Does he recognize his own limitations in judging the past? Finally, how close does he come to the past itself? These are the criteria by which this writer judges Mr. Alden's work.

One begins with the last question raised: How close does Professor Alden come to the past? There is no doubt that secondary sources are of value in aiding the scholar. But, sooner or later, the historian must identify and make use of primary sources. Perhaps, they have been stored in someone's attic. Perhaps, they suddenly turn up. But they are the remains of their day. Our ideas are only "thoughts about the past." We may never be as close to the past as were the participants. Professor Alden comes close to understanding the military aspects of the revolutionary war. In all of his chapters on warfare, he refers to primary sources. However, at other times, when not dealing with military events, he uses recently published works by secondary writers [chapter five]. In chapter six, the only reference to a primary source is on page eighty, the <u>Journals of the Continental Congress</u>, edited by Ford. The recent works are still "thoughts about the past." Unless they are backed by primary evidence they are merely interesting speculations. In the military aspects of the work, Mr. Alden succeeds as a historian. But the non-military parts have too many secondary sources and not enough primary evidence to be completely convincing.

Does Mr. Alden recognize his limitations in judging the past? There are times during the work in which the author realizes his limitations as a writer and as a historian. He cautions the reader with words like "possibly," and "probably." Even in his footnotes, Mr. Alden is careful to use these words depending upon the nature of the material he cites [chapter 4, p. 43]. He does at times weigh the evidence carefully and then presents his findings to the reader. There seem to be more "possibilities" and "probabilities" than there are "certainties." This is good since we have limitations in judging the past. We are too removed from it to be so certain of such a broad topic as the American Revolution. But, it is his synthesis, or his approach to the subject, that needs examination.

It is Professor Alden's argument that by 1775, the English government was making a mistake in trying to coerce a people 3,000 miles away. "Neither George III nor any cabinet member had ever been in America; they did not know the strength and spirit of the colonies…."[p.8]. In his synthesis, Mr. Alden implies that it was inevitable that the Americans would win their freedom. This writer agrees with a reviewer who wonders just how sure Mr. Alden is that the Americans were bound to win at the very beginning.[3] "It seemed doubtful that Britain could gather sufficient manpower to overwhelm the colonists, even with …those loyal to the king, since the American population, about two and one-half million, was more then one-quarter of that of Britain" [p.9].

In the Chapter, "Road to Lexington," the author carries his argument even further. He reaches the conclusion that the Americans were looking for war to begin. "If open warfare was not anticipated by most Americans, some nevertheless did what they could to make ready for it." [p.14]. The selection of material for the synthesis may be more clearly seen when one examines the Battle of Lexington. When so much has been written as to who fired the first shot at Lexington, the redcoats, or the patriots, Mr. Alden quotes only Major Pitcairn of the British army. Major Pitcairn's report to General Gage states "…I instantly called the soldiers not to fire, but surround them, and after several repetitions of those positive orders…some of the rebels… who had jumped over the wall fired four or five shots at the soldiers." [p. 23]. Actually, Major Pitcairn's report contradicts statements made by other eyewitnesses. Mr. Alden should not rest his case on limited evidence. This stand of the author helps to explain his choice of an aggressive portrait of the Americans at the Battle of Lexington.

It is amazing that Mr. Alden, a historian, should look back and imply that the English should have known better than to start war with the Americans. When one examines the entire work one finds the author saying that the blunders of Gage, Howe, and their British officers cost them the opportunity of winning the war. In fact, one finishes the book with the feeling that the British mistake was that her officers did not act fast enough in combat. Not once in the book does the reader encounter "smooth sailing" for the Americans, a people bound to win the war. One finds, instead, a people torn by social and economic differences, and a people tired and ill trained for war. Thus, although Professor Alden goes through the steps of external and internal criticism, his selection and evaluation of material leave much to be desired.

---

[3]Merrill Jensen, "Labor Pains of the Republic, <u>Saturday Review of Literature</u>  30 (Feb. 27, 1954) p.16.

**Part II**

Chapter seven, "Long Island to Morristown," begins not with the arrival of the British forces at Staten Island, but with the British and Tory plans in the south for a joint campaign in the middle and southern Atlantic colonies [pp.90-94]. The British government had been hoping that John Stuart, Royal Indian Superintendent in the Southern Colonies, would use his influence over the Cherokee and Creek nations to strike at the Americans. This action would help, along with the occupation of New York, to control the rebels [p. 91]. However, Professor Alden claims that Stuart was eager for neutrality between the Indians and patriots. Stuart felt this way because his wife was being held hostage in the south by the rebels and because he was against Indian cruelties in warfare [p. 91]. The author has based his remarks on a work by Mr. Philip M. Hamer.[4] Mr. Hamer, paraphrased correctly,[5] uses primary sources to support his narrative. He cites Stuart's own testimony.[6] In it, Stuart denies the charge of inciting Indian uprisings against the colonies. Mr. Hamer also mentions two additional pieces of evidence to prove Stuart's innocence. However, this writer has not examined them.[7]

Of no less importance to Mr. Alden are the Loyalists who hoped to defeat the rebels in time to receive aid from the expected convoy. Some of these Loyalists, says the author, were members of the old Regulators, the back country folk [p. 91]. These people were exploited by lawyers and real estate officials of the tidewater sections. They received help from the sympathetic British. As for the origin and complaints of the Regulators, the author correctly paraphrases the testimony of an old leader, Hermon Husband.[8]

On February 27, 1776, the Loyalists gathered at Moore's Creek and were defeated by the patriots [p. 92]. The author paraphrases Mr. Ashe's[9] and Mr. DeMond's[10] accounts of the battle at Moore's Creek. Unfortunately, Mr. Ashe offers no footnote for his version of the battle although he agrees with Mr. DeMond.[11] The latter writer does recommend an earlier published work which has not been examined.[12]

In his transition paragraph from the discussion on the South to the invasion of New York City, Professor Alden commits a professional blunder [pp. 94-95]. He paraphrases Mr. Anderson.[13] The author states that General Howe, while in New York, became convinced that it would take a long time to win the war. For such an important point of view, Mr. Alden should

---

[4]Philip M. Hamer, "John Stuart's Indian Policy During the Early Months of the American Revolution," The Mississippi Valley Historical Review, XVII (Dec. 1930) pp. 351-366.

[5]Ibid., pp 358-363.

[6]"John Stuart to the Committee of Intelligence," America and the West Indies, Great Britain Public Record Office, 1860-1953, vol. 5 (London) pp. 313-314.

[7]"Droyton to John Stuart," America and the West Indies, Great Britain Public Record Office, 1860-1953, vol.5 (London) p. 329. "Cameron to John Stuart," America and the West Indies, Great Britain Public Record Office, 1860-1953, vol. 5 (London) p. 169.

[8]William K. Boyd ed., Some Eighteen Century Tracts Concerning North Carolina (Raleigh: Edwards and Broughton Company, 1927), pp. 255, 386.

[9]Samuel A. Ashe, History of North Carolina (Greensboro, North Carolina: Charles L. Van Noppen, 1908), vol.1, p. 504.

[10]Robert O. DeMond, The Loyalists in North Carolina During the Revolution (Durham, North Carolina: Duke University Press, 1940), p.94.

[11]Loc.cit.

[12]E.W. Caruthers, Interesting Revolutionary Incidents (Philadelphia: Hayes, 1856), p. 86.

[13]Troyer Steele Anderson, The Command of the Howe Brothers During the American Revolution (New York and London: Oxford University Press 1936), p.124.

cite evidence. As it is, Mr. Anderson has no citation for his remarks about General Howe.[14] Thus, Mr. Alden is not wise in this particular selection of material.

Although generally careful with the mechanics of citation, Professor Alden makes a serious mistake [p.96]. Analyzing General Howe's desire for a peace conference with General Washington, the author explains that Washington was forced to issue a denial of the peace terms to his troops. Alden's only reference for this remark is given as The Orderly Books of Colonel William Henshaw....[15] This writer patiently examined the contents of this work, but found no such entry. Thus, for this writer, Mr. Alden's assertion is invalid.

At this point in chapter seven, from pages ninety-seven until page one hundred three, Mr. Alden's discussion centers on a map reproduced on page ninety-eight. He describes the movements of British and patriot forces and the battles which occur in New York City and Long Island. As for the map, it leaves much to be desired. For example, when this writer was reading the narrative, it was necessary to examine another map in order to understand what Mr. Alden was saying. The author mentioned the following places in his account of troop movements: Wallabout, and Gowanus Bays [p.97], Jamaica Pass [p.98], Kingsbridge [p. 100], Kip's Bay [p. 101], Harlem Heights [p. 102], and Throg's Neck [p. 103]. Not one of these locations is included on the map.

For the account of troop movements, Mr. Alden has relied heavily upon the work by Mr. Ward.[16] The author does take pains to paraphrase Ward correctly. Regarding Mr. Ward's sources, he refers to Mr. Field's work on the Battle of Long Island.[17] Again, Mr. Ward accurately paraphrases. But, Mr. Field does not document his narrative.

The makeup of the troops of General Washington at New York City is described by the author as, "largely untrained and unreliable, in service for varying periods" [p. 97]. For supporting evidence, the author cites two independent, primary sources which agree on the poor quality of personnel.[18] In the second of the two primary sources, an officer writes: "...half a dozen men have already been flogged, and thrice the number have deserved to be. I would be happy to see a good company or regiment of my countrymen in the army, but equally mortified to see it disgraced by such a set as I have got."[19]

For the surrender of Fort Washington to the British, Professor Alden blames Greene for his bad judgment and Washington for his inconsistency [p. 105]. For his authority, the author cites Mr. Knollenberg's work.[20] Mr. Knollenberg, in turn, has cited a letter from General Greene

---

[14]Loc. cit.

[15]American Antiquarian Society Proceedings, The Orderly Books of Colonel William Henshaw, October 1, 1775 through October 3, 1776, vol. 57 (Worcester, Massachusetts: 1948) pp. 16-234.

[16]Christopher L. Ward, The Delaware Continentals 1776-1783 (Wilmington, Delaware: 1941) pp 30-41.

[17]Thomas W. Field, The Battle of Long Island (Brooklyn: 1869), pp 389-390.

[18]George H. Ryden, ed., Letters to and from Caesar Rodney 1756-1784 (Philadelphia: University of Pennsylvania Press, 1933), p. 112.
Peter Force, ed., American Archives: Fifth Series Containing A Documentary History of the United States of America, vol. 2 (Washington: 1851), p. 197.

[19]Peter Force, p. 197.

[20]Bernhard Knollenberg, Washington and the Revolution: A Reappraisal (New York: The Macmillan Company, 1940), pp . 134-137.

to Washington in which Greene assures Washington that the garrison on Manhattan, Fort Washington, is in no "great danger."[21]  However, Mr. Knollenberg fails to document his conclusion that Washington was also to blame for his inconsistency.[22]

The concluding pages of chapter seven, pages one hundred six through one hundred eleven, take up troop movements and battles in New Jersey.  For his account of the battles of Trenton and Princeton, the author refers to a primary account written by a patriot soldier, John Greenwood,[23] and the secondary writer, William Stryker.[24]  Mr. Alden has again paraphrased these men correctly.  As for Mr. Stryker's documentation, he reveals the source of his information on pages 442 and 452 in the appendix.

What conclusions may one draw regarding scholarship for this chapter?  First, except for one case of faulty mechanics of citation, Mr. Alden quotes and paraphrases the sources correctly.  Second, the map is poor and of little value to the narrative.  Either a special map for the battles in New York City as well as the one presented for Long Island should be included; or a single map with the complete listing of locations should be given.  Third, and last, the author fails to use enough primary sources.  He offers too many secondary accounts, several of which are not documented.

---

[21]Ibid., p. 134.
[22]Ibid., pp. 136-137.
[23]John Greenwood, The Revolutionary Services of John Greenwood of Boston and New York 1775-1783. (New York: The DeVinne Press, 1922), p.40.
[24]William S. Stryker, The Battle of Trenton and Princeton (Boston: Houghton, Mifflin and Company, 1898) pp. 274-275; 287-288.

# Bibliography

## Primary Sources

### The Annotations Have Been Written by Jack Block

Alden, John R. The American Revolution 1775-1783. New York: Harper and Brothers, 1954, 294 pp.

American Antiquarian Society. The Orderly Books of Colonel William Henshaw October 1, 1775 through October 3, 1776. vol. 57 (April 16, 1947), pp. 16-234.

Boyd, William K., ed. Some Eighteenth Century Tracts Concerning North Carolina, Raleigh, North Carolina: Edwards and Broughton Company, 1927, 508 pp.
These are interesting to read, especially the views of Hermon Husband.

Cresswell, Nicholas., ed. The Journal of Nicholas Cresswell 1774-1777. New York: Dial Press, 1924. 287 pp.
These are the views of a young Englishman at the time of the Battle of Trenton and Princeton.

Fitzpatrick, John C., ed. The Writings of George Washington, 39 vols. Washington Government Printing Office, 1931-1944
Washington writes of his plans and goals for the war. The writings are exhaustive.

Force, Peter, ed. American Archives: Fifth Series Containing A Documentary History of The United States of America. 3 vols. Washington Government Printing Office, 1848-1853.
The entire work is filled with statements of eyewitnesses and contemporaries of the day.

Ford, Worthington C., ed. Journals of the Continental Congress 1774-1789. 34 vols. Washington: Government Printing Office, 1904-1937.
These are of value when studying the views of the Congress regarding New York and New Jersey Campaigns.

Great Britain Public Record Office. Calendar of State Papers. 42 vols. London: 1860-1953.
These contain official government views about the colonials and English officials in the American colonies.

Greenwood, Isaac, ed. The Revolutionary Service of John Greenwood of Boston and New York 1775-1783. New York: The DeVinne Press, 155 pp.

Read, William, ed. The Life and Correspondence of George Read. Philadelphia: J.B. Lippincott and Company, 1870. 575 pp.
He writes about the campaigns in and around New York.

Ryden, George H., ed. <u>Letters to and from Caesar Rodney</u>. 1756-1784. Philadelphia: University of Pennsylvania Press, 1933. 482 pp.
Rodney, a Delaware officer, writes of the hardships at New York City.

Scull, G.D., ed. <u>Memoir and Letters of Captain W. Glanville Evelyn</u>. Oxford, England: James Parker and Company, 1879. 140 pp.
Evelyn disagrees with the view that the war in New York will take a long time.

# Secondary Sources

Alden, John Richard. Who's Who in America, Chicago: Marques Publications (1899-1955) vol.28, p.37.

Anderson, Troyer S. The Command of the Howe Brothers During the American Revolution. New York and London: Oxford University Press, 1936. 368 pp. This is interesting to read, but Anderson does not document all key sentences or paragraphs.

Ashe, Samuel A. History of North Carolina. 2 vols. Greensboro, North Carolina: Charles L. Van Noppen, 1908.
  Mr. Ashe does not document his findings.

Caruthers, E.W. Interesting Revolutionary Incidents. Philadelphia: Hayes, 1856. 448 pp.

DeMond, Robert O.  The Loyalists in North Carolina During the Revolution. Durham, North Carolina: Duke University Press, 1940. 286 pp.

Field, Thomas W. The Battle of Long Island. Brooklyn, New York: Long Island Historical Society, 1869. 400 pp.
  Unfortunately, the author does not document his statements.

Hammer, Philip M. "John Stuart's Indian Policy During the Early Months of the American Revolution," The Mississippi Valley Historical Review. XVII (December 1930), pp. 351-366.
  Mr. Hammer documents fully.

James Mertice M, and Dorothy Brown, eds. The Book Review Digest. New York: The H.W. Wilson Company, 1954. p.7.
  Quotations from reviews are helpful if reviews are not available.

Jensen, Merrill. "Labor Pains of the Republic," Saturday Review of Literature. (February 27, 1954) p.16.

Johnston, Henry P. The Campaign of 1776 Around New York and Boston. New York: S.W. Green, 1878. 505 pp.
  Mr. Ward refers to this work in his footnotes.

Knollenberg, Bernhard. Washington and the Revolution:  A Reappraisal. New York: The MacMillan Company, 1940. 269 pp.
  At times the author does not document important statements.

Stryker, William S. The Battles of Trenton and Princeton.  Boston:  Houghton, Mifflin and Company, 1898. 514 pp.
He is interesting and provides footnotes for major paragraphs.

Tolles, Frederick B. The American Historical Review.  LX (October 1954-July 1955), pp. 118-120.

Ward, Christopher L. The Delaware Continentals 1776-1783. Delaware:  Delaware Heritage Press, 1941. 620 pp.
Professor Alden relies heavily upon the work by Mr. Ward.

# CHAPTER XIX

## PREPARING A HISTORICAL PAPER

No matter what special interest you have: sports, knitting, art, music, dating, there is a history to it. A history of painting, of music, or of dating, for examples, will involve use of the processes of history. Because you may find primary and/or secondary materials, you must not overlook the need for critical examination of your evidence. Suppose you want to trace the history of dating in this country. It may sound like a waste of time to some people. Think about it for a minute. By tracing how male and female behaved toward each other, you may uncover the moral view regarding courtship practices at each stage of our country's development. During the colonial period of American history, did a male and female actually date? Could the word, "date," have been understood by colonial society as we now use it?

Similarly, the work or career that you pursue has its own special history: carpentry, religion, chemistry, teaching, law, politics, military service, as well as hundreds of other occupations or professions. In this chapter, you will learn how the modern scholar examines a topic and develops it to its conclusion. Involved are the steps in preparing and writing a historical paper. The correct choice of a topic about which to write is absolutely essential to the successful completion of the paper. Otherwise, you will force yourself to do the work every step of the way. If you enjoy the topic, you will enjoy the work; such force will not be necessary.

It makes little sense to trace the history of dating from Ancient Greece to modern America. It is just as foolish to study dating from the period of British colonization in America to the twenty-first century. You will be covering so much historical ground that the scope of the topic will overburden you. There are enough sources devoted to American colonial society and its morals to involve you in research for days or months. It must be well understood that whatever topic you finally select must be <u>narrowed.</u> Some historians have written about only one day's event, such as the following: the attack on Fort Sumter, or the assassination of President Lincoln. Others have chosen as their topics a series of closely connected events such as: the civil rights movement of the 1960's, America in World War II, the United States in the 1920's. Scholars have traced specific movements covering a span of years: the growth of American labor, the transformation of the United States from nation to world power**.**

In your mind should be the question, "What is the purpose of my investigation?" In selecting a topic, examine the use of such interrogatives as: what, which, where, when, how, why, who, and whom. These words are so common in our everyday language that we take each for granted. Yet examine each carefully. <u>What</u> actually happened to Amelia Earhart? <u>Which</u> side was responsible for the attack on Fort Sumter, the Confederate or Union forces? <u>Where</u> did the "shot heard around the world" take place? At Concord or Lexington, Massachusetts? <u>When </u>did the first Africans arrive in colonial America? <u>How</u> did the Germans surrender in 1945 and under whose orders? <u>Why </u>couldn't the settlers in colonial America live in peace with indigenous tribes? <u>Who</u> was responsible for the capture of Anne Frank and her family during World War II? <u>To whom</u> should Andrew Carnegie have given thanks for obtaining work in the Pittsburg branch office of the telegraph company, to his uncle, his father, or himself? This position turned a poor immigrant boy into a wealthy man.

Perhaps, in formulating a problematic title, you should narrow the topic. Did or did not George Washington have a sense of humor? Was it true or false that Abraham Lincoln had his only romance with Ann Rutledge? Was there extensive or limited religious toleration in colonial America? This last question will show the foolishness of not carefully wording your title. Consider the extent of religious toleration granted to Jews under the reign of Peter Stuyvesant in Dutch New York. Do not overlook the treatment of Roman Catholics in Maryland, especially during the period from 1660 to 1690. What was the fate of Quakers in the Massachusetts Bay Colony during the same period? Without narrowing the scope in time, place, and action, you will be caught in a self-made trap of over-extension. The topic will become too enormous for you to handle effectively.

The next step in preparing the paper involves defining all terms in the title of the work. In the question "Why was the battleship Maine blown up?" the phrase "blown up" must be defined. Did the explosion abolish the ship completely? Did it destroy the usefulness of the ship in the war against Spain? What impression do we have from the words "blown up"? You want the reader to understand how you are going to use those words. Then, you are going to proceed to determine what actually happened to the Maine. At the same time, you will be questioning your title as you go through your evidence.

Examine a few more titles with the aim of defining all terms. Notice the following: "How much religious toleration was there toward Roman Catholics in colonial Maryland, 1660-1700?" The word, "toleration" needs closer examination. To some, it may mean the act of putting up with something that is distasteful. To others, it may signify the act of showing sympathy for beliefs or practices different from one's own. What does the word mean to you? What did it mean in 1660? Notice, also, the above title does not tell us who was doing the tolerating: the official government of Maryland, other religions, or the British government?

Next, consider the topic, "The Boston Massacre." The title has not been phrased in the form of a question nor problem. Its exact wording, however, is created by the individual writer. Again, how should we define "Massacre"? The dictionary may define it as the killing of a large number of persons. When one looks at the evidence, one finds that only a handful of people were killed. Perhaps, it would have been better for the writer to rephrase the title in the following way: The Boston Massacre, Fact or Fiction?

As our last example for this section of the chapter, let us examine the word "established." When was slavery established in colonial America? Does "established" mean the day that the institution of slavery was put into law? Does it mean the day it was put into practice by colonial society? Years may have passed in the colonies between the establishment of a system of black indentured servitude and the actual legal enslavement of people. Was the length of servitude gradually extended from five, six, or seven years to ten or twenty and then for life; or, did it happen suddenly?

At this point, you should state whether or not a problem exists. Are you able to arrive at workable definitions for all key words in your title? In the case of Abraham Lincoln, he may have lived during a period in history when people did not fall in love and then marry. Perhaps, families arranged marriages. That is, parents may have found eligible marriage partners for all daughters and/or sons. If this were true, then the word "romance" is completely  misleading in such a title as, "The Abraham Lincoln – Ann Rutledge Romance."   The author of the study which appears after the chapter, *"Reaching Conclusions,"* would have to explain that she is using the term, "romance" in the modern sense of a love story.  It is very likely that some romance could have taken place, especially on the frontier of American civilization. A young man had moved away from his home town and was looking for work in the newly developing West. Away from family restrictions and old-fashioned conventions, a youth like Abraham Lincoln was free to develop a loving relationship with the woman of his choice.

There is a difference of opinion among historians concerning the inclusion of the term, "hypothesis." Hypothesis means a provisional, tentative, working assumption, or explanation. For example, one may say, "It is my hypothesis that the battleship *MAINE* was deliberately blown up by Cuban nationalists who wanted the United States to enter a war on their side against Spain." If you examine this hypothesis carefully, you will see that the author of the statement of hypothesis has already decided on the conclusions and synthesis. Those who agree with a presentation of a formal statement of hypothesis at the start of the paper claim that the scholar will write with sincerity, strong interest, and accuracy because he or she has a reason to write. That is, the scholar has a conviction and belief that what is about to be put on paper is absolutely correct. They, also, argue that if there are any doubts in the minds of other historians about the hypothesis, let these doubters evaluate the author's work through external and internal analysis.

In opposition, those who oppose the formulation of a hypothesis at the outset of the paper have equally valid arguments. They feel that there is great danger in having preconceived hypotheses. They argue that what we should all try to do is to free ourselves from our own biases and prejudices. We must, they say, be able to work out our problem without trying to prove something, except that we are as open minded as humanly possible. Too often, the scholar who has some theory about the subject may, consciously or subconsciously, spend time looking only for sources which support his or her hypothesis. Finally, this group feels that one should phrase such a question on the *MAINE* as follows:  Who or what was responsible for blowing up the battleship *MAINE*?  Whether or not to use the hypothesis is your decision.   Above all, the choice depends entirely on the purpose of your investigation.

What is the next step in the preparation of a study? After you have chosen a topic, decided on whether or not to establish a hypothesis, defined your terms, and then stated whether or not a problem exists,  you are ready to examine the available primary and secondary sources. Where or how do you locate sources of information? Living in the information age, you are witness to the fact that a single computer chip may hold information from thousands of sources. Use the computer to obtain bibliographic information.  What is essential is that you follow the same guidelines in evaluating the materials both externally and internally for accuracy and reliability. Treat the information taken from the web as you would any other source of information. You may find that a discussion with a reference librarian on ways of obtaining sources of information will be helpful to your investigation. Feel free to examine choices with other librarians and/or teachers.

Taking <u>careful</u>, <u>accurate</u>, and <u>useful</u> notes is a crucial step in the preparation of a study. Writing notes on index cards makes most sense for both a beginner and an experienced writer. There are several reasons why you should not use regular size note paper. First, with large size paper, chances are that the pages may tear before you effectively use them. Second, you tend to become less accurate in your note-taking procedure. Finally, you tend to write too much on one sheet. Eventually, you have to cross out some notations as you make use of them for certain information. Soon, the paper may become illegible because of the many erasures and deletions.

Index cards are more durable, look neat, and are uniform in size. They may be as easily arranged as one arranges a hand in a game of cards. They may rapidly be put in any order that the writer selects. Because of their size, index cards may be placed in a pocket or purse without any difficulty. The best size to buy is the four by six inch index card. If you use a smaller size, you will not have enough space for notes. Use a larger size and you will encounter the problem of deletions. Presumably, you will not go back to your old habit of taking notes once you begin to use index cards.

Examine the handling of cards in a study. Pretend that you are doing a study on immigrants in California during the Post World War II period between 1945 and 1950. You find a book in the library which has been written by an immigrant. Having carefully inspected the work, you are ready to make use of your index cards. You will need at least three cards with which to begin. One card will be used for the bibliography, the second for taking notes. The last will serve as the reaction card for the notes you have taken. As you research library and internet sources, keep the cards separated into three packs: <u>Bibliography</u>, <u>Notes</u>, <u>Reactions</u>.

Notice example A: Bibliography. In the bottom card, the letter <u>P</u> has been printed on the top right hand corner to signify that Mr. Mueller has written about his personal experiences. Since he is an eyewitness to most of what he relates, the nature of his work is primary. On the other hand, if in 1950 Mr. Mueller had written a history of immigration during the American colonial period, obviously his statements would be secondary, the nature of the book secondary, and a letter <u>S</u> would have been printed where the letter <u>P</u> appears. Suppose that Mr. Mueller had collected letters and messages written by colonial immigrants and compiled them into a book. What letter would you print on the bibliography card? Why? Once you have written the bibliographic information, you have finished with the bibliographic card. No other bibliographic card is necessary for that particular work by Mr. Mueller. You have all the information you need in order to list this source in the bibliographic section of the study. If you have any difficulty in filling out the bibliographic card, consult with a librarian and/or study the entries provided by the library's online catalog.

Now, examine example B: Notes. Why do you suppose a question mark has been placed in the right corner of the bottom card instead of the letters <u>P</u> or <u>S</u>? Isn't the material by Mr. Mueller primary? No. It isn't unless Mr. Mueller states that he spoke with or inserted statements by immigrants who have lived in California. Nor may the letter <u>S</u> be inserted because we are not definitely told that a secondary source supplied the information.  It should be clear that even though the nature of the entire book is primary, the information given to us on page fifty-one may or may not be.  Mr. Mueller has not stated that he ever lived in California or knew first-hand the conditions of life for immigrants there.

Next, the most essential factor to consider, besides the taking of careful notes, is the sub-title.  Unless you put some heading above the information you write, you will have to read your note cards over and over in order to determine in what part of the study they belong.  If so, you lose sight of the purpose of using index cards which is:  to be able to readily find all the notes which pertain, let us say, to the "Treatment of Immigrants in California."  Remember that this particular sub-title is only <u>one</u> of many you may eventually have as you develop your set of note cards.

How do you compose sub-titles?  Very often the author gives you a good suggestion from the title of the chapter.  If not, make up your own after you have read a page or two and have decided to take some notes.  If the particular reading selection should state the causes of an event then put "Causes of…."  If a paragraph discusses results, then put "Results of…."  If it should be a personality description, what title would you give it?  Even statistics for the event deserve a title, especially when you compare numbers taken from different sources.  Try to make the sub-title heading <u>as simple as possible</u>.

The question which  always surfaces is: should one continue writing on the back of  index cards?  <u>Never</u>.  If you do, you will lessen their usefulness.  You should be able to see at a glance the entire evidence you have selected. If you have to turn each card over, you waste time and you may not easily spot agreements nor disagreements among sources of information.  Simply continue on another card or on as many as you need.  It is important that you make some notation at the top of each succeeding card that you are continuing with the same sub-title, same author, and source.

Do not forget to print the <u>exact</u> page or pages on which you found your evidence.  In the case of Mr. Mueller's book, you note page fifty-one for the remark about California.  These page numbers you write will become the basis of your footnote citations and must be carefully done.  You do not want anyone to discover some external error on your part because you put down page fifty-five when you meant page fifty-one.

Suppose, in example C, Mr. Mueller mentions on page fifty-seven that he had read a letter by a Mr. Hans Gottlieb in the book, <u>Letters by California Immigrants</u>.  Mr. Gottlieb, an immigrant living in California in 1949, states that immigrants are treated well in California.  We may expect Mr. Mueller to copy this portion of the letter, and print it.  Notice in example C, how the page references are handled at the bottom.  Why is the expression "as taken from" included in the citation?

The most difficult task in taking notes is deciding when to copy word-for-word, when to paraphrase, and when to write a few words of your own.  You should be accurate and careful in the construction of your words.  It is a good idea to copy exactly what you read if the material is primary:  letters, notes, etc. If you doubt the validity of an author's comments or if you find his or her remarks are totally different from those of other writers, you should copy word-for-word. In the reaction part of your paper you should point out any errors, or invalid statements, or prejudiced remarks. By quoting exactly what the writer has said, you let your reader see the obvious. You have changed nothing! However, for statistical information, character traits, or chronology, perhaps a few words will suffice for each note card. A final comment should be added on the taking of notes. Be yourself. Be natural. Use both the library and the computer to obtain primary and secondary sources. Then, transfer the information on to index cards.

We come to examples D, and E: Reactions to Sub-Title. The reaction card is the place at which you are most involved. Taken together, all the reaction cards form the basis of the historical criticism section of your study. Here, you must use your own words as well as imagination. How are you affected by the notes you took? Read the sample reaction cards that follow. The first refers back to Example B. Stop and think for a minute. How would you have reacted to Mr. Muller's statement on page fifty-one of his book? You may have felt that he seems to feel persecuted in the East. This may be a perfect time to examine other parts of the book on his occupation, residence, neighborhood, family, and friends. You may have felt that Mr. Muller generalizes too much about the treatment of immigrants. Is he biased? Is his language boring? Why? The above questions regarding internal evaluation could apply equally to Mr. Gottlieb who is our actual primary source in California. Notice Mr. Gottlieb's statement in example C. Now examine the second reaction card in example E. In your analysis of evidence it is important for you to evaluate whatever you wrote in the notes section; use the terms "external" or "internal" to support your analysis.

Sorting the cards, the next step in the preparation of the paper, is not a difficult assignment. However, it does require much patience and care. First, take your set of bibliography cards. Arrange them in alphabetical order according to the last name of the author. Now put them aside. Next, as in a game of cards in which you must put all the Aces, Kings, or Queens together, do the same with your note cards. To illustrate, all sub-titles on the "Treatment of Immigrants in California" should be joined. Third, arrange the different sub-titles in the order in which you wish to present your evidence. You may want to use a chronological or a topical approach. You may wish to combine both approaches. Take the reaction cards and do the same as you did with the note cards. The reaction cards on the sub-title, "Treatment of Immigrants in California" should be placed directly behind the note cards with that sub-title. Match every reaction card with a note card. Remember that the reaction card always follows the note card.

It is exciting to announce that a new process has been developed to record, separate, and store information for the three sets of cards: bibliography, notes, and reactions. The process is referred to as "bibliographic management software." This electronic process is now available through the web. This tool enables you to use any library of your choice and to transfer the information directly on to your personal computer. Some schools, colleges, and universities may have installed the software for their students' use.

At last, you come to the final step in the whole process of writing a historical study: the actual drafting of the paper. Whether you realize it or not, most of your work has been completed. By having carefully matched and arranged the index cards in the order in which you want to tell the story, you have organized your paper. Number the back of all your index cards

<u>to keep your work in order</u>.  What is most important to realize is that you are not only telling a story.  You are giving information, pointing out your evidence, and then evaluating the evidence until you have reached your last note card and last reaction card.

The conclusions of your study follow.  They are based entirely on the evidence you have pointed out and on the reactions you have made.  Use a separate index card for each conclusion you have chosen.  At the top of the card write "conclusion for the subtitle..."  Re-read carefully, sub-title by sub-title.  After you have  decided which one of the terms is appropriate: "fact," "probability," "possibility," or "uncertainty," state the one you have chosen for each sub-title and explain why you have chosen that particular word.  The conclusions, taken together, form the summary of your study.

Use the remaining index cards to formulate your synthesis or point of view.  Based upon your separate conclusions, you will have no difficulty in selecting and advancing your final comments.  Taken together, they are the answers to the questions raised in the title of your work; or they offer a solution to the hypothesis stated in the title.

**Example A: Bibliography**

| | | |
|---|---|---|
| | | **P, S** |
| **Author or Editor** | **Title as it appears** | **Primary** |
| **Last name, first** | **on inside page** | **Secondary** |
| | | |
| **Volume number (if any)** | **Publisher** | |
| | | |
| **Place of publication** | **date of copyright** | |
| **(City or town)** | | |
| | | |
| **Number of pages** | | |
| **Date of Electronic Access** | | |
| **URL** | | |

*Mueller, Heinrich; <u>My Life in America</u>*          *P*

*Brown Publishing Co., Trenton, 1956*

*pp. 251*
*(Cited, 25 September 2008)*
*http://www.Brown.com/Mueller*

**Example B: Notes**

| Author | Title | P, S, ? |
|--------|-------|---------|
| | | Primary |
| | | Secondary |

Sub-Title

<u>    Notes    </u>
_____
_____

Page or Pages

---

*Mueller*                                                                    *?*

<u>*My Life*</u>*....*

*Treatment of immigrants in California*

*Mueller writes " Immigrants who settle in California. are treated better and are accepted into American life faster than are we immigrants here in the East."*

*p. 51*

**Example C: Notes**

---

Mueller               *My Life*....                       P

*Treatment of Immigrants in California*

Mr. Mueller has quoted from a letter by Mr. Hans Gottlieb, an immigrant in Calif. during 1949. Mr. Gottlieb writes, "We immigrants are treated very well in this state."

P.57 as taken from <u>Letters By California Immigrants,</u> ed., Joan Green, Wared Publishers, San Francisco, 1950, p. 22.

*p.57*

---

**Example D: Reaction to Sub-Title, Note Card**

| | | |
|---|---|---|
| **Author** | **Title** | **P,S, ?**<br>**Primary**<br>**Secondary** |

       **Sub-Title**

            <u>**External and/or Internal Comment**</u>

       **Reactions:**

                 **page**

---

*Mueller*             <u>*My Life...*</u>                          *?*

*Reaction to: Treatment of Immigrants in California*

*(External)*
*Has Mr. Mueller talked with eyewitnesses or with people who are just repeating hearsay? I have purposely noted "?" in the notes section. I do not know whether he used a primary or secondary source.*

                           *p.51*

**Example E: Reaction to Sub-Title, Note Card**

---

Mueller                                      _My Life_

My reaction to: Letter by Hans Gottlieb                              P


(Internal)
Why does Mr. Gottlieb speak for all immigrants?  What is Mr. Gottlieb's income?
What is his Social environment like?



                              p.57

---

# CHAPTER XX

## FOOTNOTES AND BIBLIOGRAPHY

### FOOTNOTES

School and public librarians provide advice to those interested in footnotes and bibliography. This chapter has not been written as a duplication of that information. Instead, the purpose of it is to provide guidelines that you may follow with reference to historical methodology. With respect to footnoting, it is a skill and aid to clarifying, referring, and giving credit where credit is due. As a device, it should not be exaggerated nor used to over-emphasize one's research and scholarship. Good footnoting shows professional honesty and is of value in guiding the reader. It is nothing more.

There are several styles of footnoting that you may use. You may have noticed that I chose to use the American Psychological Association (APA) style in previous chapters of this text. I chose not to include the full citation, meaning complete bibliographic information. Instead, I chose to refer to one or more sources by: author(s) signature name(s), publication date(s), and page(s). What sets the APA style apart from the Chicago University style, from which the format for footnoting historical writing has been taken, is the simplicity of citation. Both writer and reader spend the least time examining citations. However, you may have noticed that I have used an adaptation of the Chicago style for all of my formal history papers for Dr. Hunt's course, "Study of History." Ms. Michalski, one of my students, applied it to her paper, "The Abraham Lincoln-Ann Rutledge Romance." The Chicago style of footnoting is well accepted as a model for studying and writing history. It will be referred to in the following portion of this chapter.

How often should you footnote evidence? There is no specific rule to follow. In general, you should not over or under-use citations. Some writers document frequently. Others, feel little obligation to their readers. It is my belief that one should footnote at least once in each paragraph. However, there will be times when you do not need to footnote a paragraph and other times when you will need more than one footnote within a paragraph, especially when you compare sources.

The first time you refer to a printed or electronic source in a footnote, you must cite the signature name of the author, complete bibliographic information, including the URL for an electronic source as well as the date accessed from the computer. Once identified in a footnote, if the same source is cited in a succeeding or later footnote, there are several ways to identify the source by using a shortened format.

Whenever you find the term, "Loc.cit." used repeatedly, you realize that the writer has been over-using this citation. "Loc.cit." is an abbreviation for the Latin phrase, "*Loco citato*," meaning "in the place cited." Because the abbreviation begins the footnote, it requires a capital letter "L." <u>Loc.cit.</u> is underlined because it replaces the name of the source that was previously cited. Not only does the abbreviation stand for the same source that was just cited, but also the same page(s). That is the reason for using the Latin term for location since the location is the page(s) cited in the previous footnote.

Now, compare the citation, "<u>Loc.cit.</u>" with "<u>Ibid</u>." There are several similarities between the two. Both terms require a capital letter because each begins an abbreviated sentence. Both are underlined because they refer to the title of the previous work and both refer to previous footnotes. However, the major difference is that in the case of "<u>Loc.cit.</u>" no page reference is needed because "<u>Loc.cit.</u>" refers to the same page as listed in the previous footnote. In the case of "<u>Ibid.</u>," it is an abbreviation of "*ibidem*" meaning "in the same place." By "same place" is meant the same source of information but not the same page. One must add the page number which must be different from the page or pages cited in the previous footnote. Here is an example of how both terms are used. We begin with footnote number five of the narrative:

[5] Burton J. Hendrick, <u>The Life Of Andrew Carnegie,</u>
(Garden City, New York: Doubleday, Doran and Company. Inc.,
1932), vol.1, p. 52. http:// etc.

[6]<u>Ibid.</u>, p. 70.

[7]<u>Loc.cit.</u>

You may also wish to use the citation, "<u>op.cit.</u>," in your writing. <u>Op.cit.</u> stands for "*opere citato.*" It means that the work has been cited in an earlier footnote. It never refers to the previous footnote as in the cases of "<u>Ibid.</u>," or "<u>Loc.cit.</u>" Because it does not begin the sentence, <u>op.cit.</u> always starts with a lower case letter "o." Since the complete citation has already been given, cite the author's last name, <u>op. cit.</u> and page(s). If there are two or more authors with the same last name, try to find some distinguishing mark such as a first name and middle initial to identify the correct author as well as the correct title.

Below, are examples of the usage of the citation, "<u>op. cit.</u>"

[8]Jack Block, <u>Studying And Writing History</u> (Westwood, New Jersey: History Publications, 2009), p.50.

[9]Hendrick, <u>op. cit.</u> p. 100.

[10]Block, <u>op. cit.</u>, p. 75.

If you discover a conflict among your sources on a particular point in question, you have to reveal what each states. It is not uncommon for there to be two or more footnotes in one sentence. As an example, notice in the following sentence how important it is to identify each source which has been used: "When the battle had ended, either fifty [7] or two hundred and fifty [8] soldiers lay dead." The two numbers indicate that a conflict exists and that two footnotes are necessary, 7 and 8.

In the chapter, *"Preparing A Historical Paper,"* the expression, "as taken from" was written on an index card. Use this phrase when you wish to disclose that you do not have access to the original source which has been excerpted in the work you have been studying. The author whose work you have been examining has given you the source of information. The writer has informed you and you have a responsibility to your reader. By adding the term "as taken from" you are telling your reader to examine the original source.

How many references should you credit or cite in one footnote? The answer depends on your aim. If you wish to demonstrate that there is considerable agreement among your sources on a particular point in question, do so by citing two or more of your findings in one footnote. Your reader will, then, understand that you have independent sources which substantiate the information you have given. If, however, your aim is to identify one source, then the footnote will contain only that reference.

Before closing this section, I should like to advise you to be consistent in your choice of style of footnoting format. If you have any doubts about the format for citations, do not hesitate to ask your librarian for assistance. Librarians are experienced in the methodology of footnoting and bibliographic notations.

## BIBLIOGRAPHY

With regard to the topic of bibliography, if you are a student your instructor may require a preliminary bibliography of works you intend to use. Here, attention is directed toward the preparation of a final bibliography which will appear at the close of your paper. When preparing a bibliography based on the processes of history, you have alternatives. You may separate works which are mainly or entirely primary from those which are secondary. You may divide sources of information into categories such as: GENERAL HISTORIES, ENCYCLOPEDIAS, BIOGRAPHIES, PERIODICALS, JOURNALS, and NEWSPAPERS, as well as other categories of your choice. Finally, you may decide to organize the bibliography alphabetically by author's last name.

Which ever method you use, a bibliography is valuable to the reader because it indicates that you have identified the evidence you have selected for your writing. In bibliographic entries, the last name of the author is given first because it is essential to identify the source of information as quickly as possible. For electronic sources, the last entry in a bibliographic citation is the URL.

In conclusion, consider annotating your bibliography. "Annotation" means that you compose a reaction that summaries your opinion of a source of information. If you choose not to annotate every source, choose several that stand out as superior to others. Place each annotation directly below the completed citation for the source. One or two sentences are sufficient. They are helpful to the reader of your study as well as to those who wish to use the references you cite in their own study or writing. The importance of the bibliography is that it enables your reader to examine the sources of your information. Also, he or she is able to see if you have consulted a variety of authors and/or editors. By noting the date of publication, you are letting your reader observe how recent or old your source is.

I am closing, not introducing this chapter, with a discussion of the purposes of your study or writing. If you choose to relate a historical incident or even several incidents within the framework of a novel or historical novel, you may not be interested in citing any evidence nor listing a bibliography of sources. Instead, you may wish to discuss your findings in the introduction or the epilogue to the narrative. On the other hand, if you choose to pinpoint an event and its historical importance to your story, it may be necessary to cite the evidence in both footnotes and bibliography. If your purpose is to examine a historical figure, you owe it to your reader to include citations. The evidence may consist of: letters, e-mail, interviews, newspaper articles, and even television or radio commentaries about your subject. These sources, if used, should be documented. Finally, whatever your purpose, enjoy the experience of putting together a work of lasting significance. Remember, footnote and bibliographic citations will only enhance the scholarship of your work.

# CHAPTER XXI

## BRIDGING THE GENERATION GAP

Never before in the history of our people has there been such a demand to question, to probe, to seek truth. We have reached the atomic age, but have much to learn about the atom's nucleus. We have begun to probe the mind to discover the meaning of personality. Indeed, investigating physical and emotional ills has expanded the range of medical specialization. In today's world of methodologies, the processes of history are essential to humanity in understanding itself and for understanding its place in history. Humanity has a need to understand its past and to question its future. The child of eight may ask, "What was I like when I was four years old?" The child of eleven may ask a parent, "What were you like when you were my age?" Similarly, in socioeconomic interaction the young are questioning their elders; the poor are questioning the rich; the deprived are questioning the affluent.

The historical investigator will share in the search for answers because he or she will be able to use special skills to inspire readers and other writers to go beyond the known or the accepted. As critical evaluation of evidence is bound to bring out inconsistency, hypocrisy, and distortion the historian will play an important role in guiding humanity through the host of fallacies that humans face in the complex world of today. In a totalitarian state, it would be impossible to question if it were subversive to the aims of a dictator. However, in the United States, we must preserve our most cherished rights to question, to inform, and to enlighten ourselves.

If we are a reflection of a complex society, we must learn how we became the nation we are and in what direction our culture is headed. The student of history will assist in uncovering the origins, sources, and importance of both tradition and change. Unfortunately, our elders often fail to realize that the future of our nation is in the hands of our young people. Furthermore, one sees a division, a wall between younger and older generations. Queen Elizabeth II sees it. In her annual Christmas message she states:

> The pressures of modern life sometimes seem to be weakening the links which have traditionally kept us together as families and communities. As children grow up and develop their own sense of confidence and independence in the ever changing technological environment, there is always the danger of a real divide opening up between young and old, based on unfamiliarity, ignorance, and misunderstanding.
> "Queen Urges Britons to Bridge the Generations,"
> The New York Times, December 26, 2006, p. A13.
> (By Permission of Agence France-Presse).

It is time to bring the two worlds together. Both generations may learn from each other by recognizing that understanding of change and tradition is essential to the understanding of history. Change need not be threatening to our elders. Nor is every tradition of the past unacceptable and useless to our young. Only if we, as students and writers of history, guide humankind in analyzing the reasons for change and tradition shall we prepare our people for the world of tomorrow. Using the processes of history: historical research, historical method, and historiography, let us challenge both generations to empathize with and appreciate each other's unique place in the continuity of history.

# BIBLIOGRAPHY

## BOOKS

Adams, James I. Atlas of American History. New York: Charles Scribner's Son, 1943.

Allen, Frederick L. Only Yesterday: An Informal History of the 1920's. New York: Harper and Son, 1957.

Beard, Charles. An Economic Interpretation of the Constitution of the United States, New York: Free Press, 1965.

Block, Jack. Understanding Historical Research: A Search for Truth. Glen Rock, New Jersey: Research Publications, 1971.

Bloom, Benjamin. Taxonomy of Educational Objectives: The Classification of Educational Goals. New York: David McKay Company, 1956.

Clark, George K. The Critical Historian. London, England: Heinemann Educational Books, Ltd., 1967.

Crump, Charles G. History and Historical Research. London: George Routledge and Sons, 1926.

Eisensehiml, Otto. Why Was Lincoln Murdered? Boston: Little Brown and Company 1937.

Elton, Geoffrey R. The Practice of History. London, Sydney University Press, 1967.

Fling, Fred M. The Writing of History: An Introduction to Historical Method. New Haven: Yale University Press, 1920.

Galbraith, Vivian H. The Historian at Work. London: British Broadcasting Corporation, 1962.

Garraghan, Gilbert J. A Guide to Historical Method. New York: Fordham University Press, 1946.

Gustavson, Carl G. A Preface to History. New York: McGraw-Hill Book Company, 1955.

Hockett, Homer C. The Critical Method In Historical Research and Writing. Westport, Connecticut: Greenwood Press, 1955, reprinted 1977.

Johnson, Allen. The Historian and Historical Evidence. New York: Charles Scribner's Sons, 1926.

Johnson, Henry. Teaching of History in Elementary and Secondary Schools With Applications to Allied Studies. New York: The Macmillan Company, 1915, reprinted 1947.

Langlois, Charles and Seignobes, C.M. Introduction to the Study of History. New York: Henry Holt and Co., 1903.

Mouly, George J. Educational Research: The Art and Science of Investigation. Boston: Allyn and Bacon, 1978.

Renier, Gustaaf J. History: Its Purpose and Method. Boston: The Beacon Press, 1950.

Rodrigues, Dawn and Rodrigues, Raymond J. The Research Paper: A Guide to Library and Internet Research. Upper Saddle River, New Jersey: Prentice Hall, 2003.

Sandburg, Carl. Abraham Lincoln: The Prairie Years and the War Years. New York: Harcourt Brace, and World, Inc., 1954.

Shafer, Robert J., Ed. A Guide to Historical Method. Homewood, Illinois: The Dorsey Press, 1969.

Stephens, Lester D. Probing the Past: A Guide to the Study and Teaching of History. Boston: Allyn and Bacon, 1974.

Stern, Fritz, R., Ed. TheVarieties of History: From Voltaire to the Present. New York: Vintage Books, 1973.

Taylor, Edmond. The Fall of the Dynasties: The Collapse of the Older Order. 1905-1922 Garden City, New York: Doubleday and Company, 1963.

Van Dalen, Deobold, B. Understanding Educational Research: An Introduction. New York: McGraw-Hill Book Company, 1973.

Vincent, John M. Aids to Historical Research. Freeport, New York: Books for Libraries Press, 1934, reprinted 1969.

Vincent, John M. Historical Research; An Outline of Theory and Practice. New York: Henry Holt and Company, 1911.

von Ranke, Leopold. The Theory and Practice of History. Indianapolis: The Bobbs-Merrill Company, 1885, reprinted 1973.

Walsh, William H. Philosophy of History: An Introduction. New York: Harper Torchbooks, Harper and Row, 1967.

**LETTERS**

Letter from Eleanor Flexner, Northhampton, Massachusetts, January 14, 1964.

**NEWSPAPERS**

Queen Elizabeth II. "Queen Urges Britons to Bridge the Generations." <u>New York Times,</u>
     December 26, 2006, p. A13.

Rutenberg, Jim and Megan C. Thee. "Poll Shows Growing Skepticism in U.S. Over Peace
     in the Middle East." <u>New York Times,</u> July 27, 2006.

**PERIODICALS**

Gibson, John S. "Legislation," <u>Newsweek Filene Center Program Current Affair Case
     Studies</u>, Medford: Lincoln Filene Center, March, 1971.

**TERM PAPERS**

Michalski, Cathy. <u>The Abraham Lincoln-Ann Rutledge Romance</u>.
     Term Paper, Fair Lawn, New Jersey: Fair Lawn High School, 1963.


Block, Jack. <u>Andrew Carnegie, 1850</u>

     <u>A Review of The American Revolution 1775-1783</u> by John Richard Alden

     <u>Coal Production In Pennsylvania for the Years 1880-1900 at Ten Year
     Interval. Graph and Design</u>

     <u>When and Where Was the First Public High School Established Within the State of
     New York?</u>
     Four papers, New York City, New York: Teachers College, Columbia
     University, 1959

INDEX

# INDEX

**A**

"The Abraham Lincoln-Ann Rutledge Romance," 58-69
Academic disciplines, in study of history, 5-14
    exercises in, 11-14
Accuracy. *See* Truth
American Psychological Association (APA), citation style, 177
Analysis, historical method and, 3
Ancestors. *See* Genealogy
Annotated bibliographies, 146, 161-164, 180
Anthropology, in historical analysis, 5-6
Archaeology
    in historical analysis, 8-9
    Tut-ankh-amun tomb excavation, 12-14
Archival materials, availability of, 81
Arnold, Sam, and Lincoln assassination, 4
Articles, as primary sources, 30
Artifacts
    interpretation of, 8-9
    as primary sources, 30-31
Art works
    criticism of, 40-42, 145
    as primary sources, 31
    as secondary sources, 35
Authenticity. *See* External investigation/criticism; Historical criticism
Autobiographical writing, criticism of, 42-43

**B**

Beliefs of historian, integrity and, 70-71, 73
Bias
    in character study, 125-127
    in genealogical research, 84, 87
    and truth, 15-19, 38, 43
Bibliographic cards, for historical paper, 168, 172
Bibliographic management software, 80, 170
Bibliographies, 145-147
    annotation of, 146, 161-164, 180
    bibliographic cards, 168, 172
    bibliographic entries, 79-81, 179-180
    criticism of, 145-146, 167-168
    preparation of, 179-180
Biology, in historical analysis, 8
Block, Jack
    "Andrew Carnegie, 1850," 132-143
    "A Review of *The American Revolution 1775-1783*," 152-164

Criticism. *See* Historical criticism
Culture, in historical analysis, 5-6, 73
Current events, 89-91

**D**
Databases, electronic, 79
Dating of events. *See* Chronology
Declaration of Independence, draft portion, 21-22
Deeds, 120
    in genealogical research, 84, 86
Dependent variables, 26
Descriptive Methodology, 28
    *See also* Interrogatives, use of
Diaries, as primary sources, 30
Directories, Internet, 79
Disciplines, academic, roles in historical analysis, 5-14
Discussions. *See* Interviews
Distortion of history, 16, 18, 70-71, 83
    internal criticism and, 39-40
    prevention of, 181-182
Drafting, of historical paper, 170-171

**E**
Ecology, in historical analysis, 8
Economics, in historical analysis, 6-7, 72
Editing, of current events reporting, 89-91
Electronic research, 77-81, 179
Elimination of information, and distortion of history, 16
Empathy, importance of, 18-19
Ethical implications, of historical method, 181-182
Evidence
    classification of, 3
    discovery of new, 28
    footnoting guidelines, 177, 180
    primary, 30-33
    secondary, 34-37
Experimentation, futility in historical analysis, 5
External investigation/criticism, 39-44, 48-52
    book review example, 152-164
    in character study, 125-127
    of electronic sources, 80
    exercises in, 45-47
    in genealogical research, 84, 86
    in historical paper preparation, 167-171
    of news sources, 89-91
    in statistical analysis, 92-94

Eye and ear witnesses, 30, 35, 89-90
    conflicting accounts, 121

**F**
Factors, definition of, 24
Facts, certainty and, 48-49, 52
Family tree, in genealogical research, 83, 88
Fiction, historical
    citation in, 180
    reviewing of, 148
Flexner, Eleanor, on locating primary sources, 33
Footnotes
    guidelines for provision of, 177-179, 180
    use and criticism of, 146-147
Foreign records, in genealogical research, 85-86
Foreign references, criticism of, 145-146
Forgery, of records, 43

**G**
Garraghan, Gilbert J., on objectivity, 23
Genealogy, 82-88
    sources of information, 83-86
Geography
    in book reviewing, 144
    in historical analysis, 8
    issues of change, 120-124
        exercises in, 122-124
Gibson, John, on governing process of society, 7
Governing process, in historical analysis, 7-8
Government offices and records
    in genealogical research, 84-87
    geographic research and, 121
Group consciousness, in historical analysis, 6

**H**
Handwriting, verification of, 43
Hear say accounts, 35
Heritage, definition of, 82
Hero worship, 127
    *See also* Character studies
Historian
    collaboration with academic specialists, 5-14
    function of, 1-3, 181-182
    integrity of, 73
    and truth, 15-22, 70-71, 73
Historical criticism, 38-47

Publication information. *See* Bibliographies

## Q
Quotation, in historical paper, 169-170

## R
Radio. *See* News media
Reaction writing, for historical paper, 170, 175-176
Reconstruction, 70-76
    in historiography, 3
    and scientific method, 24-25
    *See also* Synthesis
Recordings. *See* Voice recordings
Records
    as primary sources, 31
    reliability of, 43
Reinterpretations, 72
Reliability. *See* Historical criticism; Internal investigation/criticism
Religion
    in historical analysis, 10
    in historical study, 73
Representative samples, in statistical analysis, 92-93
Research. *See* Historical research
Reviewing books. *See* Book reviewing
Revisionist view, in study of history, 72
Rutledge, Ann, and Lincoln affair, 58-69

## S
Sandburg, Carl, conclusion terminology of, 53
Scholarship, in book reviewing, 147-148
Scientific method, and historical method, 5, 23-25, 26
Scope, of topic, 144, 165-166
Search engines, 78-79
Searching
    for prejudicial evidence, 70
    for primary sources, 30-33
    *See also* Electronic research; Historical research
Secondary sources, 34-37
    in character study, 125-127
    examination for historical paper, 167-168
    in genealogical research, 84-87
    note card citations, 168, 173-174
    *See also* Historical criticism
Selectivity
    of art work, 145
    distortion of history by, 16, 18, 70-72, 83

**U**

197